E. Kirkland

$1.50

FEW INK SCORES

While the Christian ministry is primarily a vocation, its successful prosecution depends on proper technical equipment. High ideals call for high standards in presentation. The aim of The Minister's Professional Library is to supply the modern minister with a series of authoritative books covering the professional side of his work: the actual techniques of worship, preaching, the pastoral office, running the physical plant of the church. It will present and exemplify those high professional standards which are as necessary in the ministry today as they are in medicine or law. It will include only books addressed directly to the minister in his professional capacity. It is essentially a working library which will, in time, cover the whole field of ministerial activity.

THE PREPARATION AND DELIVERY
OF SERMONS

The Minister's Professional Library

THE USE OF THE BIBLE IN PREACHING
By Carl S. Patton

PLAIN THOUGHTS ON WORSHIP
By Edwin A. Goldsworthy

THE BUSINESS ADMINISTRATION OF A CHURCH
By Robert Cashman

THE MINISTER'S JOB
By Albert W. Palmer

THE PREPARATION AND DELIVERY OF SERMONS
By Carl S. Patton

FORM AND FREEDOM IN WORSHIP
By Clarence Seidenspinner

Other volumes to follow

THE PREPARATION
AND DELIVERY
OF SERMONS

BY

CARL S. PATTON

Professor of Homiletics, Pacific School of Religion
Berkeley, California

WILLETT, CLARK & COMPANY
CHICAGO   NEW YORK
1938

'Copyright 1938 by
WILLETT, CLARK & COMPANY

Manufactured in The U. S. A. by The Plimpton Press
Norwood, Mass.-La Porte, Ind.

Second Printing

CONTENTS

5270

PREFACE

THIS is a book on the preparation and delivery of sermons. I shall say more about preparation than about delivery. However important delivery may be, the first thing is to have something to deliver. No honest preacher can deliver well anything which he knows is not worth delivering. The first requisite, even for a good delivery, is to have something to say.

I also know less about the matter of delivery, having given less attention to it. I know about it only what all men know who have tried to speak in public or have listened to other men do so. If some of the things I have thus learned are elementary, they may be all the more necessary.

What I should like to do in this book is to encourage preachers to be as good preachers as they can. Preaching is an art, and has to be learned by doing. Nobody can tell anybody else how to be a good preacher; nobody can learn it out of a book. But the experience of one man may be helpful to others. Since one's own experience is about all he has from which to learn, I shall speak as personally as I please.

C. S. P.

BERKELEY, CALIFORNIA

THE PREPARATION AND DELIVERY
OF SERMONS

Chapter One

THE PRIMACY OF PREACHING

IN MAINTAINING the primacy of preaching I do not wish to disparage pastoral work. The latter is quite too often neglected these days. Some men neglect it because it is hard work and there are other things they like to do better; some because they wish to spend all their time on their sermons. But besides the fact that people have a right to complain if they do not know their minister there is also the fact that every preacher would preach better for doing a reasonable amount of pastoral work. There is a kind of homiletic material to be got from talking with people in their homes and their offices that is not to be had in any other way. The best sermons grow out of what you know people need. You can find out what that is in a roundabout way by reading novels or studying psychology. A simpler and better way is to learn to know your people, seeing them as often, as informally, and in as personal a manner as you can.

There are other things a minister has to be besides being a preacher, or even a preacher and a pastor. He has to be, for one thing, a leader of public worship. The attention now given in our theological schools and in much religious literature to the conduct of public worship is very much to the good. Worship itself is not an art. It is the spontaneous uplifting of the soul in praise and prayer. But the soul must have wings to rise on and an atmosphere in which it can rise. To conduct public worship in such a manner as to furnish these wings and this atmosphere is one of the finest of the fine arts.

It will not do to assume that a man can fitly lead a congregation in worship just because he is personally pious. A student in one of my classes once handed in a collect beginning, "Oh God who are the source etc." I underscored the word "are." The next day his collect began, "Oh God who ist the source etc." This man is not a fair sample. But even among men who make no grammatical errors many have not been trained or have not taken the pains to train themselves in the liturgical style, which is as indispensable for good public prayers as a good homiletic style is for good sermons. This art of conducting public worship, especially in the non-liturgical churches, the minister must work at as long as he lives. What I say about the primacy of preaching carries no reflection upon it.

The minister has also, I suppose, to be more or less of a businessman. With the possible exception of the sexton he is generally the one permanent employee of his institution. He is the one man to whom the success or failure of his institution is personally most important. He cannot shirk his responsibility for the finances of his church. If it does not pay its bills he will be held responsible. If it has a balance in the bank he will sleep much easier on Saturday night, especially when the annual meeting and the end of the church year draw near. If his board of trustees lacks leadership he must be chief engineer of the every-member canvass or chief financial expert in the making of the budget. Yet these financial responsibilities he shares with other people. So far as they are well discharged by others, the less he has to do with them the better.

As to business methods either in his own work or in the management of his church, every man must find his own. What sort of filing system he wants, or whether he wants any, he will have to discover for himself. For some years after I began to preach I tried every filing system I heard of. I kept cutting out stuff and filing it away, under the impression that I must be businesslike, only to find afterwards either that I didn't know where the material was or that I didn't want it. At the end of the first twenty years of my ministry I filed all the sermons I had written up to that time in the incinerator. Nobody ever asked for any of them, and I never missed any of them myself. It is doubtless a good thing to know how reports should be made and kept. But considering how many reports have been made that need not have been made, and kept that need not have been kept, report making also is not so important as it may be made to seem. I am not advocating carelessness or slovenliness in ministerial work, either in the study or in the church. But every man must find his own methods. And methods are always secondary.

The minister these days also, especially if he is pastor of a church where few if any assistants can be employed, must know something about what to do with boys and girls. Religious education, with its training in ways of enlisting the interest of young people gathered for athletics, entertainment, hiking, woodlore and so on, is all to the good here. I recall a statement Dr. George A. Gordon made on some occasion, that in his youth, in Scotland, he never saw or heard anything in a church calculated to appeal to anyone under forty years of age. This state of affairs cannot be accounted for by Walter Pitkin's theory that life begins at forty, for it had not yet been enunciated. The change from such a situation as Dr. Gordon describes to that we now have is significant and salutary. And the minister of these days should know something of what to do with and for youth above the kindergarten age.

I pay glad tribute to all those activities by which the minister makes himself useful and beloved — and then I say that they are all secondary; are now, always have been, always will be, world without end — I would even add, " Amen." For blessed is the minister who knows that however well he may do any or all of these things, by themselves or to the impairment of his more primary function they can never make a minister. The church lived seventeen hundred years without a Sunday school. It lived a hundred and fifty years longer without a troop of Boy Scouts. Robert Chalmers never met a Friendly Indian. Henry Ward Beecher had no skill in woodcraft. Phillips Brooks was not an expert in the tying of knots or the pitching of pup tents. Dr. Gladden paid no attention to the finances of his church but let the trustees find the money. No record has come down as to what filing system Chrysostom used or what Savonarola did with his reports. The leaders of the church who have made lasting names for themselves, who have deeply affected the thought of their time and made the church a real power in human life, have never done it by any secondary or accessory means; they have done it by their preaching.

Dr. Percy Dearmer in his volume, *The Church at Prayer,* maintains that however true it may have been in the past that preaching was primary, in our time it must be secondary to other elements in public worship. We have, he says, so many churches, and therefore so many preachers, that no great proportion of them can be geniuses at preaching. But it is not necessary that they should be. A few men get into the ministry, as into all callings, who are conspicuously unadapted to speaking in public. ("Why," asked a friend of mine one day, " do all the men with an impediment in their speech go into the ministry?") There is occasionally a man with an alogical mind. In my homiletics classes I have now and then had a student of whom I have thought — probably too harshly — that if he should find a copy of *Hamlet* that had been misbound, with the last scene coming first and the first scene somewhere in the middle, he would not notice that anything was wrong with it. I do not maintain that you can make a preacher out of such a man. There is a minimum qualification for any calling. " Not every good man can keep a hotel." But any man with a naturally orderly mind and without a positive impediment in his speech can learn to put truth plainly so that people can understand it, and forcibly so that they will feel it. The eloquence of simplicity, clearness, sincerity, and absolute personal conviction is open to most men. And what other eloquence is so persuasive? What other kind will last, or is anything but a detachable decoration?

Considerable attention was recently attracted by the proposal of a New York clergyman that we " declare a moratorium on preaching." Twenty years ago when religious education was in the saddle, it was sometimes felt that it might supply some substitute for preaching. When the attention of the ministry has been especially engrossed with the "enrichment of the service," the sermon has often been spoken of as if it were the natural enemy of such enrichment. We need a moratorium on bad preaching. Religious education is as much needed for the people who go to church as for those who go to Sunday school. The better the service the more terrible to have it spoiled by a poor sermon. But neither religious education nor enrichment of the service is a substitute for good preaching. The leadership of the church is still in the hands of those who master " the foolishness of preaching."

One reason why it is in their hands is that, though there are many subsidiary things that can and should be done in the church, other people than the minister can do most of them. Only one thing he and nobody else can do, and that is the preaching. If he cannot do that he will soon have no Boy Scouts to supervise, no bills to audit, no reports to file, no anything at all. Everything depends on him as a preacher.

The real output of a church is the ideas that come from its pulpit. What people need are things to think about — ideas, ideals, convictions, thoughts that move the mind, beliefs that enlarge the soul, words that proceed out of the mouth of the Lord via the mouth of the preacher. It does not matter how many people attend the church suppers, nor how well the every-member canvass is conducted, if what comes from the pulpit is trivial, commonplace, sterile. Ideas move the world. What the editorial column is to the editor, the schoolmaster's desk to the teacher, the platform to the singer, or the stage to the actor, the pulpit is to the preacher. It is his one and only chance.

The men who have made the church by preaching have never done it by tricks of oratory. A few of them have been great orators. Most of them have doubtless had some personal persuasiveness or winsomeness that helped their message to gain entrance into the hearts of their hearers. But they have not done it by tricks either of writing or of speaking. They have done it by wisdom, knowledge, sincerity and conviction, by the substance of what they had to say.

This is not to say that the form of their thought and the manner of its delivery have had no influence. Far from it. But the men who have made the church a real factor in personal life and in civilization have done it by getting hold of truth, which when deeply felt and adequately uttered by the preacher is capable of influencing the actual conduct of men's lives. No absolute distinction can be drawn between form and substance. Someone has said, " You can't say the same thing in two ways " — because, I suppose, said in a different way it becomes a different thing. But so far as substance and form can be separated, the substance is fundamental. It is that to which we give the form and without which the form is of no consequence. The first question therefore is, What sort of material ought to go into sermons?

CHAPTER TWO

MATERIAL FOR THE SERMON

THE FUNDAMENTAL MATERIAL OF SERMONS

WHAT kind of stuff ought to go into sermons? It used to be maintained — though nobody could ever have quite lived up to the precept — that one should preach only what he had experienced. You might as well say that no doctor should prescribe for tuberculosis who hasn't had it, or no surgeon amputate a leg who still has two of his own. How little any of us has experienced when he first begins to preach, say at twenty-six or twenty-seven years of age. Even at seventy, with a whole life behind him, how small a fraction of the total of Christian conviction, practice, and hope, has passed through the soul of any individual preacher. Who has experienced immortality, for instance? Some little vicarious suffering I suppose we have all experienced, yet hardly enough to form the basis of any adequate preaching about it. We have all been saved from some things, yet most of us not from the things many people need to be saved from. We believe in the possibility of recovery from drunkenness, prostitution, and other of the worst forms of vice; yet few of us preachers have been saved from these things, or know by personal experience the pain and travail of such a salvation.

Shall we never preach about war because we have never been to war? Or about labor troubles because we have never

8

been in a lockout? Or about atheism or paganism because we have never been atheists or pagans? In some sense and to some extent we all know God and have had personal experience of him; yet whoever should restrict his preaching about God to what comes out of his personal experience would certainly preach an emaciated gospel.

Many things that ought to be preached about are not open to personal experience, certainly not to that of any one individual. I have mentioned immortality as one of these; there are plenty of others. We believe in the final triumph of good over evil, but it is not a matter open to the experience of anyone who lives in the midst of the process. One of our fundamental convictions concerns the line everywhere drawn between the evil and the good. This line we draw for ourselves largely from personal experience, yet even this not wholly. And the conviction about the primary importance of the line we get not from experience but from thinking about it. If we believe in the doctrine of evolution and regard it as a valuable revelation of the ways of God in his creation, it is not because of our personal experience, but because of what the geologists and the biologists tell us. None of us will ever experience the coming of the kingdom of God in this world, yet the conviction of its coming is an invaluable part of our Christian message.

In all these matters the preacher is only where the scientist is in his domain. No scientist has ever experienced the universality of natural law. He believes that nothing happens in the physical world without a physical cause; perhaps his whole case hangs upon this belief. But it is certainly not a thing he has experienced. All he has experienced is that he has never known such a thing to happen. What he believes about the impossibility of its happening anywhere at any time rests on grounds quite other than experience. When the philosopher teaches the objectivity of value, he does so not primarily out of his own experience.

The grain of truth in the old idea that we are to preach only what we have experienced is that we are not to preach anything that has not in some way become real to us. Guesses and hypotheses carry little weight. Speculations can never take the place of convictions. Yet even speculation has a place in all human thought, religious or otherwise, and not all convictions are reached by experience.

If we are to go beyond our own experience for sermon material, how far afield shall we look for it? I should say, as far as possible. Remembering always what a church is for, and that a sermon is a sermon and not a lecture or a treatise, we ought to preach anything that will help people. The little *caveat* I have just inserted will rule out some things. It would help people to know what automobile to buy, but there are other places where they can learn that. It would help them to know something about diet — if anybody knows anything worth saying about it; but the doctor and not the preacher is the man to give advice here. Common sense and a little tact will rule out other matters. Even some things that intimately affect the moral and spiritual life, such as sexual questions, will for obvious reasons and for most preachers have no place in the pulpit. Whoever reads John Haynes Holmes' sermon, "Sex: Are There Any Standards?" will have to admit that even this touchy subject can be treated in a sermon. But the combination of frankness and delicacy required for a profitable treatment of it is certainly not at the command of every preacher.

Aside from such exceptions as one will instinctively make, anything can go into a sermon that will help people in their spiritual life. I use the term " spiritual " because it is the most inclusive word we can use in this connection. If it is said that the preacher's message should always be a religious one I should agree, provided " religious " be taken in the broadest sense possible.

It was a dictum of Shailer Mathews' that " people come to church not for truth but for help." I suppose he uttered it as a warning against the overintellectualization of sermons, especially among young preachers. The warning is doubtless valuable even for older ones. To forget that people need help is fatal. The question is, What helps them?

Starting from Dean Mathews' aphorism it is safe to say that truth, not untruth, helps them. Yet not all truth helps equally. The truth sets us free, as Jesus said. I suppose there is no truth however remote or abstract that does not have some liberating quality. Yet the truth, for instance, that there are spots on the moon doesn't set most of us free from anything in particular. The truth that sets us free is the truth that has to do with life — with ourselves, with conduct, with human relations, with God and his attitude toward us and our duties toward him.

What helps people? First, to believe something fundamental about life and religion. The fundamental religious belief is belief in God. It is significant that contemporary theologians have largely forsaken the discussion of particular doctrines, such as Trinity, atonement, future punishment,

Christologies of any sort, and are addressing themselves to the fundamental question of theism.

The average man has not discarded his belief in God. He seeks, as yet, no substitute for him. He does not need to have God proved to him, but he does need to have God made real to him. He knows, if he reads any books, that there are people who think belief in God is passé. He knows perhaps that even in the church there is a humanistic movement which maintains that we have bothered too much about God and that we would better leave him alone for a while and see what we can do for ourselves. He knows that among those who think and write about religion there is much discussion and great difference of opinion about God. He knows that the Bible is very differently regarded among scholars from the way it was in his home town. He observes the passing of old standards of conduct, old ideas about sex and family relations, old theological beliefs. He sees all things dimly as in a flux or " like trees, walking." He has a vague idea that maybe " science " has said something that renders God superfluous or impossible. He may even have heard of naturalism, or of a new materialism supposed to be intellectually more respectable than the old one. He has lost his conviction that religion is the only foundation of morals. He knows people who do not believe in God, or who say they do not, or who at least have few or no dealings with him — people who are quite as good as many who profess a much closer acquaintance with him. It is natural for him to think that perhaps the changes that have occurred and are still occurring in religious thought have made the being of God a doubtful matter. If he lived through the World War some very serious questions about God probably rose in his mind, quite apart from any of these influences I have mentioned. Anyhow, he needs help about God.

Who doesn't? Who doesn't, even without a World War or any such contemporary questionings or disillusionments as we have recently gone through? A recent writer (I think Dr. Wieman) closes an article in one of our religious journals with the statement, "God is more than we can think." Who ever supposed otherwise? But certainly God, in so far as he is beyond what we can think, does not concern us. It is God as we can think that we have to do with. What most if not all Christian people need is to think about God in ways that bring him "home to their bosoms," as Bacon said — ways that make him real, that enable us to live in the consciousness of him and have his help and approval. They need, for the first and simplest thing, to think oftener about him.

Whoever will read Dr. Samuel Shoemaker's volume of sermons, *National Resurrection,* in Harper's "Monthly Pulpit" series, will find there a remarkably fine example of how a preacher can and should preach about God out of his own experience. Yet whoever limits himself to his personal experience with God, compelling as that will always be, will leave unsaid many things that people need to hear. Where is God to be looked for? How is he to be served? What does he want of us? What do we mean by communion with him? How have people thought of him in ages past? How and where did the prophet hear his voice? What connection has he with human life? Is he at work now essentially as he has always been?

Because the ordinary Christian hearer needs to think about God much oftener than he usually does, sermons about God, or references to God in sermons not directly concerned with him, can hardly be too frequent. If the preacher has nothing to say about God he would do better to stop and get something to say. He need not always preach specifically about God; God's name need not always appear in the title of the sermon. But whatever he is discussing he can always bring it around to God, and if it is a matter that God has nothing to do with or that means nothing to God it is not worth discussing in a sermon.

There is too much preaching about things that do not matter, or at least are not central, are on the periphery of things. What the preacher says about them may be so or may not. Either way, it makes no great difference. It is impossible to do great preaching about trivial things. But while it is not necessary that the preacher should always be preaching specifically about God, any subject is made great if he can show its bearing upon our conception of God, or its place in the plan of God for his world, or use it in any other way to make God more real to his people. To think oftener and in more fruitful and human ways about God certainly helps people, and a preacher with any skill in the avoidance of mere repetition cannot preach too much or too often about God.

Perhaps one reason why we preach less about God than our ancestors did is the fact that we do not care so much as they did for argument, and talk about God often resolves itself into argument. The place of argument in the sermon is probably not so important now as it was when salvation was supposed to hang upon correct opinions and when such opinions were considered capable of being almost mathematically demonstrated. It may be true, as Walt Whitman said, that

> Sermons and arguments never convince;
> The damp of the night drives deeper into the soul.

Yet argument, in the larger sense, is not to be despised or forgotten. For this generation it should not be what we call "forensic." It should not be too watertight, nor seem designed to push the hearer into a position against his own judgment. Nobody writes philosophy these days after the Q.E.D. manner of "blessed Spinoza," yet philosophy is throughout a kind of argument.

Some questions fundamental to the pulpit cannot be treated except by way of argument. The question of theism is conspicuous among these. The preacher who says to his congregation, "I will now prove God to you," will indeed not get far; but whatever he says about belief in God will be designed to show the place of that belief among other human convictions, to prove how far and in what respects one's total view of the universe is advanced and unified by the theistic conception, and how far short his interpretation of human life falls without that conception. However non-syllogistic its form, all this is still argument.

It is often said that the existence of God cannot be proved. It is true that it cannot be proved like a problem in arithmetic; nor can it be proved in the sense that any man of sound mind who hears the proof must be convinced. For religious purposes this is not a loss but a gain. A God who could not be doubted and in whom a man would have to believe under penalty of proving himself a fool, would not be much of a God, and belief in him would lack the moral and spiritual element that gives value to belief in anything ideal. But the existence of God can be proved in the sense that it can be shown to explain more things, and leave fewer unexplained, than any other hypothesis, and is therefore a reasonable one; that is the only kind of proof to which it is open or which is worth anything to it. For such a result the preacher should be willing and glad to argue. His people will be entirely able to understand and appreciate such an argument. Goldsmith said of his schoolmaster:

> In arguing too the parson owned his skill,
> For e'en though vanquished he could argue still.

This kind of ability will hardly win for the contemporary preacher the admiration of his more discerning hearers. But this is not the only kind of ability to be displayed in argument. No preacher need be afraid of argument rightly used. It is especially in place when one speaks of God.

Second, it helps people to know about Jesus. He is none too well known yet, even among people who have always gone to church. To be sure, God is primary, not Jesus. But in Christendom the life of Jesus, his idealism, his sympathies and antipathies, his teachings about personal and social life, what it was he quarreled with in the religion of his times, what religion meant to him, what he thought about God and man, his death and its effect upon his immediate disciples and since them upon the Christian world — anything about Jesus that is not commonplace or platitudinous is interesting and helpful to people. If it be said that these things have been repeated over and over, so have most other things that are worth saying in the pulpit. It is the preacher's business to say them with such skill and such adaptation to the life of his own times that they will not sound old.

Such preaching helps people to think of Jesus more realistically and humanly and shows that even after all Christologies have disappeared and all theories of the atonement been abandoned Jesus is still central in the Christian message. This mine of homiletic material lies mostly outside the preacher's personal experience — in the realm of history and literature. Yet it is more worth preaching about than many things he has himself experienced. It will tie up with his own experience. He will not preach about Jesus as if Jesus were only a man in a book.

Most people seldom, if ever, read the Gospels these days; and when they do they fail to draw a distinction between the Jesus of the Synoptic Gospels and the Jesus of the Fourth Gospel, and between the infancy sections of Luke or Matthew and the Sermon on the Mount. Some of them stumble a little over the miracles, or get the impression that Jesus was not quite a human being. To one reading the Gospels without help there is often a remoteness about the figure of Jesus that cuts him off from one's understanding and sympathy. But unless Christendom has grossly exaggerated the importance of Jesus in the Christian life, he is still one of the great themes of pulpit discourse. In my own judgment, so long as the preacher is a real preacher and not merely a New Testament critic, the more he knows about Gospel criticism the more humanly and realistically will he preach about Jesus. At any rate, everything helps people that leads them to an appreciation of Jesus.

I do not find myself wholly in accord with what is said in some books about "preaching Christ." I do not quite understand, for instance, what Dr. Buttrick means when he says, in his volume *Jesus Came Preaching,* that Christ is the preacher's authority. Authority for what? Authority of what kind? Dr. Buttrick explains: "The paradox of authority: a compulsion safeguarding our freedom — a finality challenging us by the unknown. . . . True authority is both quest and goal."

I wish these sentences gave me more light than they do. It is probably my own fault that they do not. But if Dr. Buttrick means that when the preacher preaches something which Jesus also said, he thus gets a guaranty of its truth, the answer is that even the statement Jesus made carries the authority (or guaranty) only of such truth as it visibly contains. If the Synoptic Gospels are to be taken at their face value, Jesus said he would come again, on the clouds of glory, within the lifetime of those who were listening to him. If the preacher declares, "I do not believe Jesus ever said that," he sets himself up as an authority on what Jesus did or did not say. If he says, "He said it, but he did not mean by it what has generally been supposed," he sets himself up as an interpreter of Jesus' statements. If Dr. Buttrick means only that Christian preachers, like the rest of the Christian world, are still under the spell of the teaching, example, and influence of the historic Jesus, that is quite true. But if he means that preachers have no right to preach anything Jesus did not say, or that when they preach anything that Jesus did say they are sure to be right, I do not see any justification for either of his statements.

There are authorities in religion as there are in physics or chemistry; that is, there are men who know more about these subjects than we do and to whose opinion we naturally defer. But this does not mean that we must accept what they say irrespective of our own judgment. I do not see what is to be gained by claiming such authority for Jesus, nor what kind of authority the preacher can find for anything he says except the truth which people recognize in it, nor why he should look for any other authority than that.

Indeed I am not always sure just what people mean when they say we must " preach Christ," or that Christ is our message. The early disciples " preached Christ " because they told the story of Jesus, and added their conviction that Jesus, through his resurrection, had become one with God, would return to judge the world, and so on. But we do not believe Jesus will come again to judge the world. We are not sure just what we mean by his resurrection. We do not see any way in which he was or could be " one with God " except the way of trust and obedience which is open to all other men. We must all " preach Christ," of course, in the sense that we draw suggestion and inspiration from his life and teachings.

Even here I do not see that anything is gained by exaggeration. It may be true, as Ozora Davis says in his *Preaching on Church and Community Occasions,* that " the wisest man cannot go beyond Jesus as an interpreter of life." But it would seem to be equally true that the simplest can go as far. Dr. Davis says again: " Christ is living now, unseen but real, actually able to make contacts with us, to reproduce his motives in ours "; and again, that we are to seek the springs of the highest joy and the sources of the noblest living " not in a record of Jesus but in the living Christ "; and once more, that " Jesus is still the living Master of Souls."

Such statements are undoubtedly the utterance of personal conviction backed by religious experience. But it is at least open to men who use such language, if not incumbent upon them, to explain in what manner Jesus lives today — what manner other than that in which Shakespeare or Beethoven lives — and what is the relation of the living Christ to the Jesus of the Gospels and to God. I hesitate to say it, but I do believe there is and has been much thoughtless exaggeration about Jesus. I would not endorse, but I would recommend a reading of the chapter entitled " The Jesus Stereotype." in Harry Elmer Barnes' *Twilight of Christianity*. I would not dwell much upon the somewhat bizarre experience H. G. Wells recounts in his *First and Last Things,* in which after trying in vain to be responsive to the Jesus of the Gospels he finally finds a " savior " in Oliver Goldsmith. About all that can be deduced from this is Mr. Wells' desperate need of a savior of some sort — because if Goldsmith would do, almost anybody would. But I would give much more weight to the statement of a sober-minded and discriminating man like Professor Charles Cooley, who in one of his volumes says that he has never received as much help from the personality of Jesus as from that of some other men. Perhaps he is saying here only what many others would say if they thought it proper to do so.

However that may be, he certainly " preaches Christ "

who preaches the gentleness, the humility, the confidence in God and in humanity, that are conspicuous in the historical Jesus. This is not a book on theology, and I do not wish to get into any argument about Jesus or the living Christ. I wish only to indicate that in what is called "preaching Christ" there is room for much intellectual discrimination. However earnestly the preacher may claim Christ as his authority, his own words, whether about Christ or anything else, will carry only the authority of such good sense as people can find in them. And this brings me back again, with all the more emphasis, to my statement that to know more about Jesus certainly helps people.

It helps them too to have their difficulties removed. These are of many sorts. Some of them are practical, like the following: What can be said for Christianity in a world that is no better than this after two thousand years of Christianity? The answer has sometimes been that Christianity has never been tried, but that answer won't do; it only leads to a more difficult question: What can be said for a religion that has been in the world for two thousand years and never even got itself tried? Are the Christian nations any better than the non-Christian? The World War was not a Buddhist nor a Mohammedan war, but a Christian one. Just what is the superiority of Christianity to other religions — if it has any? Granting that what we call Christian civilization is in some respects superior to the non-Christian civilizations, is it possible to say how much of this superiority is due to Christianity and how much to other causes?

Some questions which people raise concern the church rather than Christianity as a system of belief and practice.

Why is the church so slow to appreciate social progress or to take sides with the underprivileged? Why does it so often seem to be merely a conservative force resisting all progress? Why has it damned the scientists, excommunicated the philosophers, burned the heretics? There are answers, not merely excuses and apologies, to all such questions. To the man who knows the history of the church and of human thought and progress in general, there are answers as satisfactory as can be given for any of our human failures and shortcomings. These answers the average churchgoer does not know. There is no reason why he should know them. They lie largely outside his reading and thought.

Some intellectual difficulties are of a broader and more general sort. What do we mean by faith, which we are always exhorting people to have, and how does faith differ from guesswork? Is there a sixth sense by which we know God, or do we know him by the same processes of experience and reflection which guide us in other realms? Is there anything left of the old idea of providence? What has become of the other old doctrines, and why after lasting for so many centuries have they in our own time gone so utterly to pieces? If they are not true now were they ever true? If they were ever true why aren't they true still? What do we mean by truth in religion? And how do we get it or test it? Not everybody asks such questions, but some folks do, and more would if they had more help from the pulpit toward answering them.

People have many difficulties about the Bible. What are they to believe about the events narrated in it, events so utterly unlike those of today? Miracles, for instance. What shall they make of a history like that of the exodus, where it is said that several million people get together and move out of Egypt in one night at the blast of one or two trumpets, drink out of one well, assemble before one " tent of meeting," and immediately after their deliverance from slavery have enough gold, silver, precious stones and rare tapestries to stock an entire second-hand section of a modern city? What are they to do with the nonmoral or even the immoral parts of the Old Testament narratives? Or with the conception often revealed there of a God who is capricious, vindictive, or childish?

It is not, for the most part, young people of an age to join the church who are troubled about such matters. Young folks generally accept religion because of its idealistic appeal. It is the more mature persons who ask questions about it. If such people have any real religion they are not likely to give it up on account of these intellectual difficulties. But unless they give up reading the Bible (which most of them do) or forget entirely what used to be read to them out of that book, such questions give them an uneasy feeling. Are they perhaps believing in things they cannot defend, things which no sensible adult can easily believe in? To answer them is part of the function of adult religious education, carried on from the pulpit by the preacher. People will rest more easily and solidly in their religion if such questions are answered and such difficulties removed. And this is one thing, subordinate but still important, that sermons can do.

It has been implied that educative preaching helps people. The Christian religion has had a long history, the spiritual life of the race a much longer one. How much do ordinary churchgoers know of all this? If you ask, "How much do they need to know?" I answer, "Nothing at all if your only interest in preaching to them is to get them into the church and keep them there." But if you feel that, in religion as in other spheres, the more intelligent we are the better the results, it will not be necessary to argue with you that any preaching which broadens people's acquaintance with Christianity, or with the larger spiritual history of which Christianity is one chapter, does them good. If it be said that most people have no intellectual interests (I believe it was Dean Hodges who said he once counted seven bishops asleep in one congregation), is it not part of the business of the preacher to awaken an intellectual interest in Christianity? Most of us think, when we are given something to think about that seems worth while.

It does people good to be shown the bearings of Christianity upon the practical problems that press upon the world. Most of us want to do right, if we can only be sure what right is. Few of us are without sympathy for the multitude of people who do the world's hard, uninteresting and ill-paid work and from our standpoint get so little out of life. We read of strikes, lockouts, wars and preparations for wars, of governmental experiments like those of Russia, Germany, and Italy, of race relations and race hatreds. However little personal responsibility we may have for any of these matters, if there is a Christian way to think and feel about them most of us want to find it.

These things come under the head of the so-called "social gospel." They do not lie at the center of personal religion, but for any man who seeks something more than the salvation of his own little soul they certainly come within its circumference. There is no conflict between personal and social religion; they are not things between which one has to choose. Personal religion of the right sort is the strongest single motive to social action. A personal religion that leaves its owner content with all the immemorial wrongs and injustices of the world is almost, if not quite, contemptible. It never does leave a man so if it is religion of a deep and thoughtful kind.

We are here in a realm where differences of opinion and attitude are many and sharp. Here the preacher has need of all the skill and patience and good sense the Lord has given him. Businessmen will not be told by preachers how to run their business. The military minded will not be converted to pacifism by sermons, however subtle and persuasive. But if there is any feeling about the world's social, economic, and international troubles, and any one attitude toward them which is more obviously and adequately Christian than another, it is only fair to assume that at least many Christian people can be brought to entertain this feeling and assume this attitude. Any preacher who gives up the attempt to bring people to this attitude and feeling has shirked an important part of his duty. He has made it easier for the church and for individual Christians to live for and within themselves, and has made religion a smaller thing than it should be. Intelligent and sensitive Christian people want help in these matters, even though they may sometimes be very touchy about them.

It also helps people to be put into a good mood. Indefinite as this may sound, some people sometimes need it more than

they need to be instructed on some tangled question or urged
to some difficult or unwelcome duty. They come to church
disgusted with themselves and with the world. They are
tired, nervous, overstrung. To be shown the plight the world
is in and to be urged to do their duty is exactly the thing they
do not need. They need to be quieted down, cheered up,
shown that in their own lives and in human society not
everything is a hopeless mess. They need spiritual recreation.
One does not preach sermons like Burris Jenkins' "Knee
Deep in June" or "The Dropped Bridle Rein" to bring
home any new truth, nor to urge to any particular duty, nor
to reprove for any particular sin, but to put people into a
mood which enables them to live more easily with themselves, their families and their friends. The bow that is always stretched loses its elasticity. People can respond until
they can't respond. I seem to remember the instance of a
woman who got nervous prostration because at her church
they sang too often, "Rise, my soul, stretch every nerve."

I have probably said enough toward indicating how wide
is the field for sermon material, and how far it extends beyond the sphere of any merely personal experience, however
often it may start from or come back to that. What I have
said raises several other questions.

The first is, How much truth is there in the old contention
that the preacher should always "preach for a verdict"? He
often reproves himself for not doing so. It is a common criticism of him on the part of others. He is sometimes compared
with the lawyer, who is supposed always to talk for a verdict.
Must the preacher always do likewise? No! When he is
urging people to join the church, or to make public profes-

sion of religion, or to do any other particular and specific thing, then he will "preach for a verdict." He will push for it as hard as he can. But he is not a lawyer; he is something much more inclusive and human than that.

Does the singer sing for a verdict, or the poet write for one, or the painter paint for one? In a vague and intangible sense perhaps they do. They are not without hope that what they sing or write or paint will have some influence upon human moods or thought. If so intangible a thing can be called a "verdict," they work for one; and so does the preacher, no matter what he preaches about. But if by a verdict you mean a "yes" or "no" to some specific demand, or even a course of conduct immediately and radically altered, not all sermons are preached for a verdict, or should be. The preacher is, like the poet or the painter, an interpreter of life. He is an artist in the things of the spirit. To limit him to preaching for a verdict would make him a smaller man than he now is.

In a recent magazine article Dr. Fosdick contended that preaching should be "life-centered," not "Bible-centered." Quite so; except that folks in Bible times were alive also, and the Bible is the great source book of religion. The life in which preaching should be centered is not merely that which is going on at this particular moment. Preaching should not be science-centered, nor philosophy-centered, nor literature-centered. Yet science, philosophy, and literature are also part of life. Education should not be curriculum-centered but pupil-centered. Obviously the object of all preaching is to interpret life, to illuminate it, to improve the quality of it. One cannot accomplish this if he loses sight of life itself, or draws his materials ultimately from any other or smaller source. But life is not merely lived within us and around us. It is mediated to us in art, in science, in philosophy, in literature, and in religion itself as a historic process. If a man is human enough to be in the ministry at all there is no danger that his preaching will be other than life-centered.

Considerable attention was attracted recently by a statement of Reinhold Niebuhr's that "moral" preaching leaves people cold. I suppose that depends on who does the preaching. Certainly much of the preaching (if it should be called preaching) of Jesus was moral; that is, it had to do with how people ought to behave. It is not easy to draw the line between moral preaching and preaching that is something more than moral. Matthew Arnold's definition of religion as morality tinged with emotion is not a good one, but it is suggestive. Religion ought at least to be tinged with morality, though it has not always been. The Christian church is not an ethical society, but conduct — ways of behaving, morality — is certainly part of its province. I suppose the sermon already referred to, John Haynes Holmes' "Sex: Are There Any Standards?" would be called a moral sermon; yet it would hardly leave anyone cold, nor would it seem trivial to anyone who heard it. I assume that a preacher who wishes to preach upon a moral question will know how to show religion's bearing upon it. Religion is not a hod carrier to morality; it exists in its own right. Yet there is no moral question whatever upon which religion does not throw its own light.

Should a preacher avoid controversial subjects? Yes, if he wants to hold his job with as little trouble as possible and doesn't care about his personal influence; no, if he wants to influence people either in thought or in conduct. A naturally contentious preacher easily makes a nuisance of himself. A man who hunts for controversial topics, who enjoys them more than any other kind, and who can make a controversial topic out of almost anything, belongs in the boxing ring rather than in the pulpit.

But many times the livest topics are those most in controversy. There is hardly a topic that is not controversial at some point. There may be no controversy about the golden rule as an abstract proposition, but there certainly is controversy about where it ought to be applied and who ought to apply it first. To avoid controversial topics, theological or social, through fear of raising differences of opinion, and so to speak only of things upon which everybody is agreed, is like hunting in a forest where all the game has already been killed — neither profitable nor exhilarating. To discuss controversial topics requires skill, patience, modesty, art, and especially love; but how can a man who has not at least a modicum of these requirements preach on any topic at all?

Which brings up the question of freedom in the pulpit. One hears ministers complain occasionally of a lack of such freedom. The constraint, where it exists, now concerns social and economic rather than merely theological questions. In churches which have felt any liberalizing influence the preacher nowadays may unburden himself of almost any purely theological heresy, short of absolute humanism, without serious protest from his congregation. Of many churches, of course, this is not yet true, but even where it is true there is still frequently pressure upon the preacher to keep to purely personal or spiritual matters, and so away from social or economic matters. Yet in the long run, if he will take his time and not annoy his people needlessly or continuously, the preacher gets his liberty even at this point. No congregation of sensible people wants its preacher hampered in the utterance of truth. As soon as they begin to suspect that he is suppressing his honest convictions, or saying things just because the people want them said, he loses their respect and interest.

His freedom, where it is lacking, is a thing the preacher has to win. Nobody can present him with it. He must gain it by patience, by moderation, by endless good humor, by an obvious love for the people to whom he speaks, and by a frank recognition of their right to differ from him. The liberty of listening belongs as much to the congregation as the liberty of speaking belongs to the preacher. The preacher will never win freedom of speech by refraining from speech; neither will he get it by making himself unnecessarily obnoxious concerning matters in which people differ from him. Some preachers, it must be admitted, can say things with which people agree in a way that raises their ire, and some can say things with which people do not agree in a way that makes them listen and think. At all events, and in most instances, the preacher who has anything to say will get all the liberty he knows how to use, and more than that much would be wasted on him.

Concerning this matter of the social gospel: the man who comes around to it occasionally, and "drops his word" — as Amaziah said to Amos — about it incidentally, provided he expresses his conviction clearly and fearlessly, accomplishes more than one who makes it his sole and constant theme. If a man has no message but the social one people cease to listen to him; they say, "He's hipped on that subject." But if he preaches about many other things as well, sooner or later he will say some things that appeal to his people as true. His reputation outside the realm of social questions will become good with them. They will begin to say, "He has plenty of sense in other matters. Maybe there is some truth in what he says about social questions." Moreover, when a pronouncement upon social matters appears as an incidental but essential item in a sermon dealing with something more personal or spiritual, if the rest of the sermon carries conviction it is likely to carry the social pronouncement with it. I am not urging concealment of one's social convictions, nor even caution with reference to their expression; but there is the danger of hammering away at people so continually on this or any other theme that it merely sets them against one, whereas another method gets in under their guard with unwelcome but necessary truth.

SECONDARY MATERIAL OF SERMONS

I have mentioned some things I think are fundamental in sermon material and some reasons why I think they are so. But obviously there is much more that goes into sermons. In an individual sermon what one does incidentally and on the side is sometimes quite as valuable as the main point at which one is aiming, and in the long run and over a period of years it becomes still more important. A member of the First Congregational Church of Columbus once told me that all he knew about English literature — and he knew a great deal — he had learned from Dr. Gladden's sermons. Yet Dr. Gladden never preached about English literature; whatever he said about it was incidental.

The minister is not primarily a littérateur, nor a historian or philosopher or art critic. But culture is part of the spiritual life. Whatever enlargement of the intellectual horizon the minister can communicate to his people, whatever quickening of interest in questions that engross the attention of the thoughtful, whatever refinement of taste, is a direct contribution to their spiritual life. Any ten men graduated at the same time from theological schools of the same type, and reading over a period of ten years the same sort of books, will entertain substantially the same theological opinions and the same social outlook. The fundamental things that go into their sermons will be very much the same. They will differ from one another in their skill of expression and in their power as public speakers, but still more, and more importantly, in the kind and amount of incidental material that goes into their sermons.

There are not many great religious ideas — certainly not many in the mind of any one man, preacher or otherwise. That God is our Father, that Christ is our Saviour, that the Holy Spirit is our Guide, that love is the law of life, that the human soul is immortal, that we must have as soon as we can get it a Christian world to live in — one can add a few other great religious ideas to these, but the total is soon enumerated. One can state all of them in a single sentence or put them into one sermon. To these great ideas one returns again and again, and whatever he preaches will be related to them in some way. To make these fundamental ideas real to people, to fit them into people's thought so that they will stay there, to drive them home, they must be reinforced, buttressed, illustrated, and come at from every possible angle.

The golden rule, for example, is certainly a fit subject for a sermon. But one cannot improve upon Jesus' statement of it. To prove its truth is superfluous. One can complain that people do not keep it and exhort them to do so, but that is soon done. What then shall one say about the golden rule to make a whole sermon? That depends upon what he knows about Confucius and Hillel and their similar law of conduct, about Immanuel Kant and his categorical imperative; on what he has read of various attempts to apply the rule in social and economic life; on what he knows of the self-regarding and the other-regarding motives; on his ability, in short, to bring to the support and enforcement of this simple rule an abundance of material from many realms. So it is with every other subject, simple but profound, on which he wishes to preach; so it is with his preaching over a period of years. He will not merely have announced those great principles of life and conduct which are the substance of all good preaching, but he will have set these into a rich background of human thought and experience.

Where does this incidental or secondary material of preaching come from and of what does it consist? Some of it comes from the preacher's own experience. When I was a young man and read a sermon by an older man in which there were no anecdotes, no references to history or literature, no allusions to science or philosophy, and yet plenty of matter, I would say to myself, "He has ample material here and yet he doesn't seem to have got it from anywhere outside himself." When I looked for the same kind of stuff in myself I could not find it. Even when I would take a text or a biblical passage and try to " think " about it, the thoughts that came were few and far between and not always of a quality to cause me to rejoice. I later concluded that this was because I was still too young. I hadn't lived enough. I hadn't tried enough, done enough, succeeded and failed enough, watched other people and tried to help them enough, hadn't been saddened enough or rejoiced enough, or done anything else enough — just hadn't lived enough.

Thoughts rise spontaneously in us. But they do not rise out of nothing; they rise out of experience, reflection, the wear and tear of life. Things that happen to us sink into us and form a well out of which we can draw. But it takes a long time for this well to fill up. If you try to draw something out of it when there is nothing there, what do you naturally get? When a preacher's subject is almost wholly objective, no matter how young and inexperienced he is he can get important and appropriate material from the newspapers, the current magazines, the Bible or other books. But when the subject is largely of the stuff of life itself he has to wait for life to give him his material. That is why preaching grows easier as one grows older. That is also why, when a man gets to be fifty, there are a depth and intimacy and a personal character to his preaching which it did not have when he was thirty.

Not all sermons need to come out of a man's soul, but when one does come from there it is usually better than those that come from any other source. Even when a man preaches about something largely external to himself, like war or other public or social matters, some part of his sermon — the conclusions he draws, the advice he gives — will come out of his own soul. And he can't get even these out of himself except as his experience of life has put them there. "Knowledge comes but wisdom lingers." Even knowledge doesn't come too fast or too easily, but you can hurry it up, and when you need a piece of it that you don't happen to have you can go out and get it. But wisdom, it seems, has to come to you with the years.

Aside from the material that comes from experience, where does the rest come from? Mostly from study and the reading of books. In a world such as ours, which has run so riotously to print since the time of Gutenberg, this could hardly be otherwise. Early in his process of self-education Lincoln once said, " The things I need to know are written in books." And he added that the man who could show him the right book was his best friend. It is the advantage of the ministry over most other professions that almost any book that anybody ought to read is a good book for the minister.

But I said " study and the reading of books " to indicate that these are not identical. It is a great advantage to the minister to have studied something, not merely to have read about it — I mean not only while he was in the theological school, but after that. To any man who makes a real success in his calling, ministerial or otherwise, what he has learned in even the best school is valuable chiefly as a start for what he learns by himself. His very liberty to read whatever he will, and the fact that he can hardly read anything that will not be of some value to him, may tempt the minister not to study anything.

If he is to be not merely a reader but a student, he will naturally study something germane to his work and message. Even that limitation leaves him a very wide range. He may choose some aspect of scientific thought, especially one that touches the history of the human family, like the doctrine of evolution. This doctrine has now become almost a dogma. The scientists are all for it. Anyone who has sympathy with modern ideas can see at once how out of place among them is any theory of special creation. The preacher may accept the doctrine of evolution upon these simple grounds. But if instead of merely accepting it he will make a study of it, giving to it all the time he can spare for a period of, say, two or three years (even less would do), he will find the whole idea of evolution taking a new place in his mind. If he is a wise preacher he will not obtrude it upon his people in unnecessary or obnoxious ways. He may seldom or never mention it by name, but it will have a solid standing in his mind which it did not have before, and in a subtle, perhaps largely unconscious, but powerful way it will color all his thought about the past and future of the human family. It will give him a new slant upon ethics and upon theism. Incidentally it will have furnished him with a vast amount of illustrative material for sermonic use and will enable him to speak about many things with an assurance which he would otherwise not have. To have made a thorough study of one important subject, and to know more about it than most folks, will add considerably to his self-respect. An old Greek professor, famous in his day, used to give three reasons for studying Greek. The first I have forgotten; the second was that it enabled a man to read Greek literature; the third that it gave him a sense of superiority to those who had not studied it! I wouldn't lean too heavily upon this third reason, but in a world full of specialists and in a profession whose intellectual interests are likely to be altogether too scattered it is not to be despised.

One may take some period of religious history, like the Reformation or the Puritan period of New England, and make himself an expert on it — not an expert as compared with a professor of history, but at least as compared with the average layman or even the average preacher. If he will forego for a year or two the reading of miscellaneous contemporary stuff upon which many of us spend so much time, and give himself to such a study, he will see the religious history of the world and many contemporary religious questions in a new and illuminating light. He will have a kind of *pou sto* solid under his feet. He will not see everything from his new lookout and he will not stand there all the time, but some things he will be able to see as other men do not see them and as he himself would not see them from anywhere else. There are too many preachers who do not know any one thing well enough to give them a particular advantage.

A literary period will do almost as well as a religious one. One of our New England preachers, who entertained no thought of being anything else, made a detailed study of English literature in the Victorian period. It was only an incidental result of this study that he was called to a professor's chair. More valuable results were the respect he won in his community, his own consciousness of having done something worth while and acquired a standard for measuring the rise and fall of the flood of contemporary literature, the stimulation of his own thought by intimate acquaintance with the great minds of a generation, and — never to be despised — an abundance of sermonic suggestion. An American preacher, for many years secretary of a great church organization, is an authority upon Wordsworth. His familiarity with that great poet undoubtedly accounts in part for the equanimity with which he spends his time in railroad stations and in poor hotels, and also for the refined but rugged literary quality never absent from his public addresses. One might study a contemporary literary movement, either in prose or in poetry, with equally good results. It is a good thing now and then to study something, and not merely to read books.

Study will doubtless be most profitable to the preacher if its subject lies close to religious life — the Old or New Testament, for instance. The Old Testament contains the history of religion during the most important period of its development among that ancient people that had the greatest genius for it. It is the richest single source book of religion that exists. Every theological student learns something about it, but most do little with that knowledge and say little about that book after they have become ministers. The average student gets just enough knowledge of the Old Testament to enable him to go on to a real study of it if he so desires, but not enough to be of much use to him unless he goes on. Many, however, far from continuing their study, even forget what little knowledge they did get in the seminary. This is as if one should run to the end of a springboard, pause, and then crawl back again.

I bear grateful testimony to the knowledge I acquired in the classroom of one of the greatest American Old Testament scholars, Professor George F. Moore. Yet the greatest thing I got from him was an impetus to go on and learn more for myself. All I learned in this way was, to be sure, but a fragment of what he could have told me had he had time to tell me and I sense enough to take it in. But all real education is self-education, and what I have learned of the Old Testament outside the classroom has been worth much more to me than what I learned even from a great scholar, perhaps for the reason that what I learned by myself I learned because I wanted to know it and not because it was in the curriculum.

I can hardly overcome my surprise at the number of preachers who seem content with what they learned about the Old Testament in the classroom; many of them, however, make no use even of that in their pulpits. The higher criticism has made the Old Testament a new book for the preacher, and has turned into homiletic material vast sections of it which formerly were barren waste. Since I have elsewhere * written at length on this subject I will not labor the point here. But it seems to me so important that I cannot refrain from mentioning it. We want to make our people as intelligent as possible about religion; for this purpose nothing is more valuable than a knowledge of the history of religion.

The same may be said with equal cogency of the New Testament. The preacher can use it effectively in the pulpit even though he is not versed, for example, in the synoptic

* In *The Use of the Bible in Preaching,* one of the volumes in " The Minister's Professional Library."

problem or in form criticism. How he can use it with any great consistency if he draws no distinction between the Synoptics and the Fourth Gospel is not so easy for me to see. The Jesus of the Synoptics is not the Jesus of John. The teachings of the synoptic Jesus are as different from those of John's Jesus as is one of Dwight L. Moody's sermons from one of Phillips Brooks'. How far congregations can or need be instructed in such matters is another question, but certainly a knowledge of them, as expert and thorough as he has time to gain, gives the preacher a feeling of confidence in his presentation of New Testament matters and vastly enriches and deepens his own appreciation of the greatest of all Christian books.

Again, the same thing may be said for church history. A New England woman once asked her pastor, " Didn't anything happen between the Book of Acts and the landing of the Pilgrim Fathers? " Something certainly did happen, and it may serve the preacher well to know what it was. But more important for pulpit purposes than the history of the Christian church is the history of Christian thought. "The critique of dogma is the history of dogma." When the preacher knows how every doctrine that has dominated men's minds has arisen out of some intellectual stress and ministered to some spiritual need, and how it has endured as long as it answered these purposes and disappeared when it no longer served them, he has a perspective which will relieve his own mind, as well as his parishioners', from fear about current shiftings of religious opinion. But to gain such an advantage he must have some definite knowledge of the development of Christian thought. It is not enough to know that Christian thought has developed; it is not enough to state the fact in a single sentence or even in a single sermon, else it will easily be overlooked and soon forgotten. But repeated over and over, as occasion offers, and illustrated by concrete historical instances, it will have great influence in liberating lay opinion about religious doctrine.

Finally, one other subject should be specifically mentioned — one which will abundantly repay study — that of philosophy. Theology nowadays is largely philosophy; indeed as distinct from philosophy there is not much theology left, at least in liberal circles. Among teachers in our theological schools theology now largely reduces itself to theism, and theism is a philosophical question. The pressing religious questions of the day are two: Can we get, or can we at least hope for, a decently Christian order of society? and, Is the universe capable of a spiritual interpretation? The first of these is a practical and sociological question, the second a philosophical one. There are those who maintain that religion can exist without being related to any interpretation of the universe. Probably so, but it certainly is much more natural and easy and at home in a universe where values are more than human inventions and where the human struggle for the good has some support in the character of ultimate reality.

Upon this matter many preachers, to be sure, will be content to trust to traditional thought backed up by religious experience, their own and that of others. Such a procedure is perfectly proper. But if one wishes to think about theism it is obvious that he must think philosophically. It is equally obvious that some types of philosophy lend themselves to, or lead directly toward, a theistic interpretation of the world, while others look away from such an interpretation, if they do not make it almost or quite impossible. Naturalism is perhaps the one type of philosophy which is not to be reconciled with some sort of belief in God.

No preachers, one may assume, with the possible exception of the left-wing humanists, are naturalists; and practically no philosophers are naturalists. But there are many men, some educated and some not, who though they are not out-and-out philosophical naturalists are yet under the impression that a purely natural, physical, material explanation can be given to everything in heaven and upon earth, including what we have always called the spiritual life of man. They are impressed with the fact that mind, as it appears in us, is always connected with a brain and a nervous system. There cannot be thought, so they think, where these are not. They argue something like this: To the best of our knowledge, brain and nervous system exist only in one little corner of the universe; there was a time when they had not appeared even there; there will be another time when they will have disappeared; hence mind is not merely confined to its own little corner but is a latecomer and a temporary guest. Since God, whatever else or more he is, must at least be mind, there is not much chance that he exists in a universe which has in it no mind except that which we human beings possess. If mind, however, is a characteristic not of us alone but also of the universe out of which we have come, there is at least a chance that God exists.

I do not imply that most Christian people, or even most of the people who are puzzled or in doubt about God, have clearly stated these alternatives to themselves; but they are dimly affected by the issues involved in them. Those who have read a little recent philosophy have been assured that the old "idealism" has passed. Many of them, however, will not know what aspects of idealism have really passed, nor what other types of philosophy allow a sufficient place for mind in the universe, nor how much of what is religiously valuable in idealism survives in forms of philosophy which at many points are at war with it.

Nor do I mean that people in general should be instructed in philosophy and its technique. What I would say is that some type of philosophy which leaves a natural place for God is essential to the preacher. He may of course abjure all such problems, merely taking the belief in God as part of our religious inheritance, and if he is ignorant of the questions modern philosophy raises about God he will for practical purposes be secure enough in this position. Even so, however, he can hardly escape the suspicion that things have been said about God which he ought to know, and this suspicion will hardly make his own conviction of God more firm.

There are subjects, then, about which the preacher should not be content merely to read, but which he should definitely study. This is a treatise on preaching, and I mention study here because of its importance in furnishing the preacher with sermonic material. To study carefully almost any period of history or literature, or almost any phase of religious experience like conversion or mysticism, will greatly enlarge the scope of the preacher's material and will give him in his pulpit utterances an assurance which he would otherwise not have. But the subjects which come closest to religion, like the Old and New Testaments, the history of Christian thought, and psychology and philosophy, are most worthy of study — philosophy I should say most of all, because it comes closest to the question of theism which is the battle-ground of present-day religious thought. But if his study is to be of real benefit to him the preacher must not merely know in general what is being said; he must arrive at some conclusions which to himself at least he can intelligently defend.

This is not the place to indicate in detail how this study is to be carried out. Every man will generally find his own way. However, speaking of philosophy, and by way of suggestion, I might say that almost any general history of the subject, provided it is not written in too popular a style, is a means of getting a background and a start. After that, among the books that can hardly fail to interest as well as instruct, are such as W. E. Hocking's *Types of Philosophy,* C. E. M. Joad's *Guide to Philosophy,* or J. B. Pratt's recent volume, *Personal Realism.* These are not necessarily better than scores of others, but they are easier to read than most books on philosophy. Yet once one becomes really interested no literature is richer or more fascinating than that of current philosophy.

Aside from material that has to be gathered by study there is a vast amount the preacher can gain by the simpler process of reading — reading for pleasure or appreciation, reading to put oneself in rapport with the world's great spirits, reading for no specific reason except that one wants to read. Let him read what he wants to, what he gets pleasure from, and the more he reads the more his taste will develop. And whatever the preacher reads, it will furnish grist for his mill. To be sure, much of what he reads may never appear as recognizable " material " in his sermons. He may make use of few or many quotations or allusions to history, poetry, fiction, or biography. Nevertheless, his reading will color and enrich all he says. There is something about the speech of a man who has read widely which distinguishes it from that of one who has read narrowly, something there also which is lacking in the speech of one who has studied a few things carefully but has neglected a wider field. The difference is felt even if one does not stop to analyze or name it. The well-read preacher is like a traveler who has visited many places, not only the one he is talking about. He is like an artist who has seen not only his own pictures and those of his teacher or his school, but has looked often and long at the best pictures in the world. It would be impossible, for instance, for Dr. Lynn Harold Hough or Dr. Glenn Atkins to hide the fact that they have traveled widely " in the realms of gold." Their minds have a texture that is gained only by contact with the best minds that have been.

I have talked about reading and study as sources of material for sermons. It remains to be said, as Dr. J. Edgar Park remarks in his stimulating volume, *The Miracle of Preaching,* that a preacher may come close to spoiling his own reading, and to a smaller degree his study, by being forever on the lookout for homiletic material. Let him study a thing because it is worth being studied and because he wants to know about it. Let him read what he enjoys reading, what quickens his mind and feeds his imagination and satisfies his soul. What "inures" to him, as Walt Whitman says, will come out in his preaching.

Here perhaps is the proper place for a plea for scholarship in the pulpit — for scholarship in some special field, such as Dr. Rauschenbusch had in the social sciences, or Dr. George A. Gordon in philosophy, or Dr. Wm. E. Barton in a special period and about a particular character in American history; and also for the more general type of scholarship which consists in familiarity with the history of human thought and its expression in the great literature of the race.

The scholar is not always a good preacher, but it is never his scholarship that hinders him from being one. The ministry is traditionally reckoned as one of the learned professions, and on the whole it has sustained this reputation fairly well, though perhaps not so well in some times and places as in others. In the old days in New England the preacher was not only a college and seminary man but in his general intellectual accomplishments he ranked high with the other professional men of his community — lawyers, doctors, and teachers. It has, however, not been easy to keep up this standard, particularly in the churches that are democratically governed, whose congregations have practically complete control over the selection of ministers, and in small churches, unable to pay respectable salaries and located in over-churched communities whose general intellectual standard is not too high. Besides, there are so many things other than intellectual ability that count — and rightly — when a church selects a preacher — his personal manners and address, his ability to manage things, to get along with people, and to speak well in public.

But religion is a great subject— not merely a great practical force in the conduct of individuals and of the community, but a fascinating subject for the study of any man once he has become interested in it. The history, literature, and philosophy of religion constitute a theme in comparison to which most fields of scholarship are small and restricted. Much is needed in the pulpit besides scholarship — much personal conviction, much human sympathy and understanding, much skill in public speech. But these and similar qualifications being presupposed, nothing will commend the Christian pulpit to thoughtful people more than genuine scholarship. There is perhaps a reasonable amount of it in the outstanding pulpits of the country; it is in fact one thing that makes them stand out. But in the American pulpit at large, irrespective of denomination, there is, to put it conservatively, plenty of room for more scholarship.

CHAPTER THREE

THE STRUCTURE OF THE SERMON

I HAVE dealt thus far with the material for the sermon; but when one has the material, the next question is, What is to be done with it? The treatment of this matter falls under two heads, structure and style. The first concerns the arrangement of material, the second the literary form in which it is cast.

About the simplest and most universal principle applicable to all the arts is that of unity. Whether the work of art be a Greek vase, a lyric poem, a song or a sermon, it must have unity. This principle is more important in its negative than in its positive application. A perfect work of art, presumably, will have everything in it which ought to be there. But any work of art is instantly and visibly marred by having in it anything which ought not to be there. The practiced eye will doubtless sense the absence of something whose presence would add to the unity of the whole. But even the unpracticed and uncritical sense will detect and resent the presence of anything which should be absent. What mars any story or play or sermon, any work of art whatever, and in a fashion most noticeable and obnoxious, is the presence of the superfluous.

The good preacher will ruthlessly apply this principle of unity, especially in its negative aspect. He will not permit himself to say anything in a sermon just because it is beautiful or pathetic, or because it displays his literary power or his knowledge, or for any reason other than that it is an indispensable part of the work of art he is trying to construct. I know how lovely, to the ear of the preacher who has created them, are some things which are really superfluous, and how it hurts him to leave them out. However, nobody but the preacher knows what he has left out or how lovely it was, and he may take comfort in the fact that its omission has therefore caused his congregation no pain.

The structure of the sermon would seem to require but little comment. When one speaks on any topic there is a form into which his thought falls naturally — what we call its logical form. This means merely that what ought to come first does come first, what ought to come next does come next, and so on to the end. If one has a logical mind he will arrange his material in this way without special effort. The sermon will come to him and shape itself logically in his own mind. But various degrees of logicality inhere in different minds, and perhaps such sense of logic as anyone possesses can be educated or stimulated.

To be sure, there is not always only one logical arrangement for a given collection of materials, but among various equally logical arrangements one may be more artistic and forceful than the others. In the college debating society, for example, we were told that if we had four or five points the best was to be saved for the last, the next-best presented first, and the poorer ones sandwiched in between. The weaker points would help fill up time; for some hearers they might add a little strength to the argument; and at the worst they would be placed where their weakness would be as little noticeable as possible.

This rough-and-ready rule assumes that there is no logical necessity for one point's following another; the sequence is a matter of choice with the speaker. In respect to some sermons this is true, and the sermon is not necessarily a poor one on that account. I may want to speak, for instance, on "The Homely Virtues." Among these virtues are faithfulness, economy, patience, sympathy, cheerfulness. I may arrange these items in any way that suits my purpose. There is no logical reason why one should come first, another second, and so on. I will probably find the right way of arranging them by considering the purpose I have in speaking of them. Or perhaps there is no better rule than the old one I have mentioned: to begin well and finish strong. If a speaker fails to catch his listeners' attention at the start he will find it hard to secure afterwards; and on the other hand, the point best remembered is the one last heard.

There is no obvious reason, for example, why the material in Spurgeon's sermon, "Songs in the Night," should be arranged as it is. Spurgeon's arrangement is as follows: First, who is the author of these songs in the night? The author is God himself. Second, what is the matter contained in these songs in the night? It is generally the day that is past or the day that is to come. Third, what are the excellences of songs in the night above all other song? They are hearty, they show faith and love. Fourth, what is the use of songs in the night? They cheer one's self, they encourage others. Spurgeon closes with the solemn reminder that "there is a night coming in which there will be no sense of joy," and so on. It was not logically incumbent upon him to arrange his four points in this order. The same conclusion would have followed equally well upon any other arrangement. Or one might have preferred to put the point of the songs' authorship last instead of first, thus leading up to the idea of God as the inspirer of men even in their darkest hours. This sort of material — and we all use much of it in our sermons — lends itself to such arrangement as is suggested by the conclusion the preacher wishes to draw from it. But there is other material, more intrinsically logical in character, of which this is not true at all, which must fall into the right order, just as must a story or a play.

The first law with a sermon, as with anything else, is to get a good start. Since the thought in a sermon should progress it should begin with something from which it can move. Since it should rise it should begin on a level from which it can soar, for if it begins at the climax there is nowhere to go but down.

There are other reasons for beginning as simply as possible. The congregation is made up of folks of all sorts, young and old, wise and foolish, educated and uneducated. They see every subject from innumerable angles. If they are to move off on a common path they must first be got together. Therefore it is necessary to begin with something whose truth is universally and readily recognized. It is the custom these days for the preacher to announce his topic in the Saturday or Sunday paper, or even on the previous week's church calendar. But I have never found that people pay much attention to such announcements; at least I am sure that they do not sit down and think about the preacher's theme. They appear before him on Sunday morning not only with many different kinds of mind but preoccupied with many different topics, the only principle of unity among these being the negative one that they are not the topic on which the preacher is to speak. Under these circumstances the sermon's opening sentence or sentences accomplish all that can be asked if they focus the attention of the people on something that gets their minds together. It is like the bunching of the horses at the beginning of a race.

Not all preachers will feel that this kind of preparation is necessary. Thus Bishop Slattery begins a sermon on " Keeping the Faith " with the sentences: " What does it mean to keep the faith? How shall we use the great Christian confidence which we have received from our fathers, that to the people who shall take our places we may pass it on with vigor and enthusiasm? " The listener finds himself *in medias res* from the start. I am far from saying that this method is not all right, if it is the way one prefers to begin; though I should think that some of the hearers might feel as if they had been rather rudely jerked or spurred into place and put into their fastest stride with more speed than was natural.

Most preachers, I have found, will begin a little more easily. When Dr. Sizoo begins his sermon, " The Luck o' the Road," with the words, " I was sitting one afternoon on the sun deck of a transatlantic liner homeward bound," or his sermon, " To Those Defeated," with the words, " One evening some years ago I was sitting before an open fire in the home of a friend " — one feels as if he had been eased into the subject rather than plunged into it. A beginning similar to these but more dramatic is that of Dr. John Howland Lathrop's sermon "To the Perplexed": "I can see her now as she came into my study; eighteen or nineteen years old, and on her face a puzzled, half-frightened look." With such a beginning one is not faced immediately with the problem to be discussed; he is, as I have said, " eased into it," and eager to know what is to follow.

It is probably not often that one can naturally begin a sermon in so dramatic a manner as this. What one can do is to start with some general proposition. So Dr. Poteat begins his sermon, "The Compulsions of Brotherhood," with the statement, " Brotherhood has achieved the dignity and succumbed to the fate of being an axiom." My only criticism upon this opening sentence — if I have any — is that it might not be sufficiently clear to all hearers. For a first sentence it perhaps implies too much. Nevertheless I like it; and picturing myself among the congregation I say to myself, " This man has something to say." I like still better the way the same preacher begins his sermon, " The High Cost of Conduct": " I affirm and am prepared to support the statement that the most dangerous bit of nonsense to which the moral conscience of the race has committed itself is that the best things in life are free." Spoken not too rapidly, and with a pause at the end to give it time to soak in, that introduction should open not only the sermon but the minds of the listeners. This is an example of what I had in mind when I spoke of the need for beginning with a general proposition.

Sometimes one wishes, not to plunge his hearers into the midst of his thought at one swoop, but at least to state clearly what the central contention of his sermon is to be. So Dr. Walter Russell Bowie begins one sermon by saying, " The message of this sermon can be summed up in a single sentence. It is this: Wanted, more and better Fundamentalism." He begins another sermon with, " I want to speak today to the discouraged," and another, " Here is the picture of a man who thought he could make a religion out of odds and ends." John Haynes Holmes begins one of his sermons, " I want to speak to you about the meaning and significance of religion." In any case, let us agree that few things about a sermon are more important than its beginning.

Perhaps the one more important thing is the ending. Most conclusions are too brief. To impress people properly with any idea, it is not enough to state it clearly or beautifully; one must repeat it often enough and long enough to let it sink into their minds. Twenty-nine minutes of sermon and one minute of conclusion is not a good proportion — not if it has been a real sermon from which a real conclusion can be drawn. Dr. Atkins states that one should put as much work into his conclusion as he puts into any other portion of his sermon, though the other portion be three or four times as long.

I raise one question about the conclusion of the sermon — one prompted by so many published sermons: Is it well to close with a verse or more of poetry? Every man will have his own feeling about this, of course. I can only say that the poetry should be very brief, or very good, or very pat, or even all three together, to justify its use. In general, I do not like the use of it, and I do not believe most people do. Quotations are too impersonal. To use them as a last word is to behave like a host who, when the time arrives for saying good-night at the end of a party, hands his guests over to the hired man — a left-handed, almost absent-minded perform-ance. Unless there were some extremely good reason for it, I wouldn't turn my congregation over to somebody else for the last word. Many good preachers do it, some habitually; but I have often lopped the poetry off at the end of some good strong sermon and considered the sermon improved thereby; or I have added a few words such as might naturally have come from the preacher, thus giving him the last word as well as strengthening the sermon.

What has been said about closing with poetry brings up the question of the use of quotations in the body of the ser-mon. Since this is rather a matter of style than of arrange-ment of material it will be treated later. To go back to the matter of arrangement: After one is well started there may be any number of diverse but equally good ways of develop-ing the theme or arranging the material.

The text may suggest the arrangement. For instance, the text, " Ye shall know the truth and the truth shall make you free," suggests that the truth is something that can be found. This idea lends itself to passing comment on skepti-cism, agnosticism, and other negative attitudes toward truth; perhaps to a brief discussion of whether we know religious truth in the same way we know other truth, or whether there is a special spiritual sense by which it is known; certainly to mention of the fact that in religion as elsewhere we owe noth-ing to the men who think there is no truth to be found or no way of finding it, but everything to those who have be-lieved it could be found and have done their best to find it. What follows upon this, both from the text and from the subject matter, is the fact that all truth seems to have a liberating power; all truth, no matter how abstract or remote, sets the discoverer free from something. But some kinds of truth have more liberating power than others. The truth that sets us free in matters of character and conduct is the truth that has to do with life. Religion has to do with life in its most fundamental and far-reaching aspects.

The conclusion to such a line of thought will naturally be that religious truth is not a thing to be afraid of, but a thing to be sought in the confidence that it can be found and that it will set us free. If one has not forsworn the word of exhortation, an appeal to one's hearers to search for the truth will bring the sermon to a natural conclusion. Of course one may preach on this text and follow some other line of thought; this development is not necessarily better than any other. But it is hard to see how any other could be so naturally suggested by the text itself.

In the development of so simple a line of thought as this it is immaterial whether the preacher informs his hearers at the start of just what he intends to do. The road is so straight that none can lose it in any case. But in a more complicated course of thought it is of great advantage to let people know what one is going to do. They need all the help they can get in listening. They need to know not only where the preacher begins and where he proposes to go, but from time to time how far he has progressed on the road. The lawyer says to the jury, " We shall prove, etc. From this we shall go on to show, etc.; and before we are through we hope to convince you, etc." Following a similar outline preachers used almost always to divide their sermons into sections numbered 1, 2, 3, etc. (sometimes, alas, up to 15 or 16), and close with a " finally." One may say that such chopping up of a discourse decreases its literary quality, and that people should be able to follow a sermon without such helps. A sermon, however, is a literary performance only secondarily, and people need all the help the preacher can give them.

One advantage of biblical preaching is that the material almost necessarily falls into a natural or logical order. By biblical preaching I do not mean "expository" preaching, where the preacher takes a passage and merely explains its meaning; nor do I mean preaching from a text, which may not be biblical preaching at all. I mean rather the type of preaching where one takes some incident or story from the Bible, such as that of the plagues in Egypt or the revolt of Absalom, and preaches both from and about it. In so doing he usually retells the story in his own words, making as he goes along comments that will clarify the happenings for his hearers. As the story develops logically so do his comments upon it.

One's conclusion — or so one would like to think — is so natural and necessary an outcome of his discussion that it should not have to be announced, but should be instinctively felt as such by the listener. Many things however do not seem so simple and inevitable to the hearer as they do to the speaker, and if one's sermon has been a little long, possibly a little difficult or even a little tedious, the simple word "finally," or the phrase "in conclusion," or "all this comes to the following conclusion," or something of that sort, may often be a great help to the audience and gain for the conclusion a hearing it would not otherwise receive. Some man who has been listening indifferently, fearing the sermon was never going to come to an end, will prick up his ears and say to himself, " He's going to quit, is he? Well, I guess I'll listen from now on. It can't be long, and he'll probably do his best." If he gets no such warning he is likely to say to himself afterwards, " If I'd known he was getting near the end I'd have listened. The conclusion is the whole point, and I don't like to miss it, but I didn't know he was getting to it." Indeed the conclusion often is, and generally should be, " the whole point." The preacher would prefer to have it driven into the minds of his hearers by the accumulated force of all he has previously said, but failing that he would do better to get it in by itself, and therefore to let people know when he comes to it.

The same thing holds true of other parts of the sermon and of their relation to one another. It cannot be too often repeated that what holds people's attention in a sermon is movement. Nobody looks long at a train that is standing still, but it is almost impossible to take your eyes from one that is moving. I once asked a preacher about a colleague of his and he said, " He is a bright man and has lots of ideas, but there is no movement to his mind." " No movement to his mind " — rather a handicap to a preacher, one would think. Unless the preacher has such a static mind his thought will always have movement. What he says in one part of his sermon will belong to that part and not to any other. His " thirdly " will grow out of his " secondly," as the duel in *Hamlet* grows out of the quarrel between Hamlet and Laertes. But the movement of thought in a sermon is not so obvious as the movement of action in a drama. Often the movement of the preacher's thought may be perfectly clear to him but not at all clear to his listeners; he must, therefore, make it obvious. Any love of literary form which prevents his doing so is mere pedantry. What the sermon requires is not only movement, but perfectly obvious movement. It is of no use for it to go if people can't see it go.

I have already said that the preacher who announces his course before he embarks on it helps people keep track of what he is saying. In the case of such a simple outline as I have suggested on the text, " Ye shall know the truth . . . ," such an announcement is probably superfluous. Yet I am often impressed with the value of it in a sermon whose thought and outline are both very simple. In a sermon to which I once listened, based upon a parable of Jesus that has been much misinterpreted, the preacher began: " In the treatment of this parable I shall do three things. First, I shall call attention to some things often found in the parable that are not there. Second, I shall speak of some things that are there but are generally overlooked. And third, I shall make a few remarks of my own." Listening to the sermon, I could not fail to be aware when the preacher got through with one division and passed to the next. I once heard a sermon upon the supremacy of the spiritual, in which the preacher announced at the beginning precisely what he was going to do. He was, he said, going to maintain that the spiritual always is supreme; not that it ought to be supreme, but that it is supreme in human life, even in human life which we do not always recognize, or which does not always recognize itself, as spiritual. He then said that this was the whole contention of his sermon, which he would proceed to illustrate and drive home in various ways; after which he would draw one or two simple conclusions. Nobody who listened for the first few minutes could be in any doubt as to what he was aiming at, nor could anyone who listened throughout be in doubt as to the bearing of what was said later upon what had been said to begin with.

There are other sermons in which one does not wish to announce his main purpose at the start, but rather to begin with more general matters and let the particular truth he wishes to bring home break upon his hearers like the sun through the mists. A plan of this kind is doubtless best for some topics. Besides, in the interest merely of variety, one should not always use the same method.

I recall, for example, another sermon I once heard, one on the apparently abstract topic of "Value," which was constructed in the manner just mentioned. The preacher began with the simple statement that each one of us recognizes some things as beautiful and some as ugly, some as good and some as bad. He proceeded to show how this process of evaluation is inseparable from life, not by an abstract statement to that effect but by concrete illustrations of how we unconsciously and unavoidably make evaluations every day. He next inquired whether there was any standard of value aside from individual taste or opinion. Having proved to his satisfaction that there was, he went on to the philosophic doctrine of the objectivity of value, though he did not use this terminology. He then recurred to the common observation that there is no value apart from some mind or spirit that can evaluate. The conclusion of the sermon issued naturally from what had been said. The preacher declared that, unless we are willing to think that the universe was without value and therefore without any reason for being until man appeared and would be again without value or meaning after man had disappeared (an assumption he easily made to appear somewhat ridiculous), there was no escape from the belief in an infinite or universal mind for which the whole process has value. He had thus begun with one of the commonest experiences of everyday life, that of preferring some one thing to another, and had ended with a novel and effective statement of theistic belief. As I remember, there was not much of an obviously logical skeleton to this sermon — no 1, 2, 3 arrangement or demarcation. But there was such an obvious dependence of each step in the thought upon those already taken, and such an ascent from the commonplace to the significant, that at the end one felt he could hardly preach on this subject at all without doing it in exactly the same way. The delivery of the sermon of course can do much toward bringing out the logic of its development; but of this more in another place.

What I am here insisting upon is that progress is of the essence of a good sermon, as it is of the essence of a good tale, a good play, or a good speech of any kind; that this progress must be upward as well as onward; and that it not only must be there but must be obvious. In a volume full of practical homiletic wisdom entitled *Pulpit Mirrors*, Dr. E. H. Byington remarks, " The sermon that is equally good all through is steadily losing from the start." This is well said; but it does not mean that there should be anything in the sermon that is not good enough to be there; it means that movement in mood and feeling and structure is essential to gain the interest of the hearer. When material is arranged so as to have this movement it is logically arranged. But let me add that not only the sermon as a whole should rise to a climax; every one of its divisions should do so. The sermon which arouses the hearer more at the middle than at the end is badly arranged.

Dr. Byington's remark means also that some material and moods belong in one part of the sermon but not in another. I have often been asked what place humor has in a sermon and have always answered, "No place at all, unless God so made the preacher that the natural and almost necessary way for him to say some things is the humorous way; no place at all, if the preacher consciously produces it for the sake of effect, or if he can avoid it; no place at all in the treatment of ideas or beliefs that are coarsened or lowered by it." Yet there are some things that can be said more pointedly when they are touched with humor, and it seems a pity to lose this advantage — especially if, as I have said, God made the preacher humorous to start with.

At a dinner one Saturday evening I once met a preacher of Scotch descent who kept the table in an uproar with a succession of Scotch stories told in a charming brogue and accent. After the dinner I remarked to one of this man's parishioners, "How delightful it must be to have such a man for your preacher." He looked at me blankly for an instant and then said, "He's delightful this evening, yes; but tomorrow in the pulpit he will be the driest man you ever heard." This reminds one of what Johnson said when Boswell remarked that Sheridan was naturally dull. "Yes," said Johnson, "Sherry is naturally dull; but he must have attained his present state of dullness by persistent effort. Such dullness as he now exhibits is altogether beyond nature." The fact that this was unfair to Sheridan, who does not seem to have been dull either by nature or by effort, does not affect the point. A man may throw away in the pulpit some gift of humor or sprightliness or humaneness because he thinks it is out of place there, whereas if he would use it with judgment it would add much to his power. There is no reason why a preacher should be, in Chesterton's phrase, "instinctively witty but intentionally dull." When someone asked Spurgeon at one of his services, "Can a man be a Christian and play in a brass band?" and Spurgeon answered, "Yes, but the man who lives next door to him can't," he did what no man without a natural sense of humor could have done by his most serious effort.

The advantages of humor in the pulpit are obvious: it rests people; it gives them a chance to shift the position of their bodies and the muscles of their faces; it opens up their minds so that any gem of truth or any appeal to sentiment wins an easy entrance; it is a foil against which the more serious or even solemn portions of the sermon stand out as they should. Where everything is serious, nothing is serious. Even so, humor does not belong everywhere in the sermon — never where it jars, of course, and practically never in the closing portion. The man with a humorous turn of mind is easily suspected of levity. In the early part of his sermon, while he is still in the outskirts and not at the citadel of his topic, levity can be permitted. But to introduce humor or allow it to creep into the final solemn words of his discourse, is to stamp himself a mere joker.

Negative statements also belong in the early part of the sermon. These may often be very important. We teach by contrast. It is frequently necessary to clear the ground before one can put up his own structure; but one should not still be clearing the ground in his concluding sentences, nor bring in at that place things which he wishes to warn his hearers away from. The negative statement is a springboard from which to jump, and one should not be found still poised on it when he should be at the end of his swim. So of all provisos, of all hypotheses stated for the purpose of being denied or discarded, and naturally, of all statements whose value lies in their use as an introduction or a foil to something that follows. One should always finish strong.

Pathos is a different matter, and seems to belong to either the beginning or the end of a sermon. It is doubtless more appropriate at the end, for one wishes to dismiss his hearers with their emotions stirred and their hearts warmed for kindliness, appreciation, or duty. It is occasionally appropriate at the beginning, when the speaker wishes to open his listeners' minds wide for the reception of his message. A good instance of this use of pathos is the introduction to Dr. Lathrop's sermon, " To the Perplexed," which I have quoted on page 53. In the middle of the sermon, where it is not necessary as a mind-opener and where its effect will almost surely be buried under much material that follows, pathos would seem to be largely wasted.

There is another difference between humor and pathos. Humor creeps into a sermon because the preacher has a humorous soul; pathos comes in only at the demand of the circumstances. If humor is used more freely in sermons than it once was, that is perhaps an indication of the loosening up of pulpit conventionalities and the more human character of contemporary preaching. If pathos is less often resorted to, that may indicate that modern preaching appeals more to the thoughtfulness and less to the emotionalism of the congregation than it has sometimes done. But both humor and pathos are double-edged tools, to be used only when necessary and only by those who know how to use them.

These matters of the sermon's movement and the use in it of humor and pathos evidently are as much a question of style as of the arrangement of material. The next chapter will take up the subject of the sermon's style.

CHAPTER FOUR

STYLE IN THE SERMON

THERE IS no radical distinction between a sermon and any other kind of public discourse, except for the place where and the circumstances under which it is given and the subject matter with which it deals. There is no "sacred rhetoric," no special way of writing or speaking a sermon, no peculiar homiletic style. All the principles of style which apply to a sermon apply equally to public discourse in general.

The style of speaking or writing which appears at any time in the pulpit is essentially like that which appears at the same time outside the pulpit. Around 1825, when Thomas Chalmers, in his sermon on "The Expulsive Power of a New Affection," employed a sentence of some two hundred words, other contemporary speakers and writers were doing the same sort of thing.

It must also have been at about this time that Sir Walter Scott was writing: "The sun was now resting his huge disk on the edge of the level ocean, and gilding the accumulation of clouds through which he had traveled the livelong day, and which now assembled on all sides of him like misfortunes and disasters around a falling monarch and a sinking empire." That was a noteworthy sentence, or I should not have remembered it from my days in grammar school till now. But it is not the way we say it these days.

We say, " The sun was setting." That Miles Krumbine begins his sermon on Paul in Rome with a paragraph of nine sentences, the longest of which contains seventeen words and the shortest but six, indicates not merely that the speaker is that kind of speaker but also that the present style of speaking is that kind of style. As the preacher naturally uses the vocabulary of his own day and not of some other, so he falls naturally into a style that belongs to his own time.

What this style is in our day is indicated by the comparison just made between Chalmers and Krumbine. The tempo of our life is fast, not to say jerky. The entire religious service takes less time than the sermon used to have for itself. The shortness of the sermon reacts upon its vocabulary and style, as well as upon the mood of the listeners. People today will hardly have patience or know how to listen to a preacher whose leisurely, orotund, well balanced periods suggest that he is in no hurry to get through. They not merely want him to get through on time, they want him to act as if he were going to. When they see him sail gloriously past a half dozen stopping places they get the feeling that he will never stop anywhere. We are seldom leisurely about anything these days. With a change of one word Shakespeare might have written:

> Like as the waves make toward the pebbled shore
> So do our ministers hasten to their end

The sermon is not only shorter than it used to be; even within its briefer compass it must move faster.

I am not complaining about this. In fact I consider it altogether to the good. It is not well for a public speaker to feel that he has all the time he wants. The time limit placed upon him should teach him to eliminate what can be spared and to say things in the simplest and briefest way. If he learns this lesson he can often accomplish in twenty-five minutes what took Dr. Chalmers an hour. Anyhow, the multiplicity of our engagements, our speed in getting to and away from them, the many more things we crowd into any one day or hour than our fathers did, the auto, the air mail, the telephone and the radio, the increasing proportion of our daily life that has to click with something else that will not wait — all these have reacted on the tempo of the sermon as on everything else. They have led the preacher to substitute the short sentence and even the short word for the long one, and to make his sermon a drive rather than a stroll.

A very simple matter, yet not unworthy of attention, is this of the length of the sermon. Ian McLaren might seem to have settled it once for all when he said that time had nothing to do with it; that a sermon that seemed long was long, no matter how short, and one that seemed short was short, no matter how long. But that is not quite all of it. There should be a certain reasonable proportion between the length of the entire service and that of the sermon. The softest church pews are seldom luxurious, and besides people have engagements to meet even on Sunday. It is good advice to give a young preacher — the old one may need it more but he cannot take it — to beware of the habit of speaking too long. It is a habit that grows upon a man terribly. If he speaks too long while he still has but little to say, how much more too long will he speak when he has the experience and wisdom of many years to utter!

It is not so easy to be more specific about this matter. But perhaps I should say that twenty-five minutes is a good time limit for a young preacher, with thirty as a more absolute one. If he begins at twenty-five he is likely to go up to thirty-five or forty; if he begins at forty he will never get back to twenty-five.

There is one danger in this short and fast-moving sermon. A certain elevation of style is not merely appropriate to certain subjects, but is demanded by them. The modern preacher is apt to feel that he has no time for this. He is wrong about that. He has time for it wherever it is required; and he will hardly fail to take time for it if he is at heart anything of a poet, or if the routine of his ministerial life and the disillusionments of his calling have not killed all sentiment in him.

There is a charming passage of this leisurely sort in a sermon by Dr. Atkins, "The Land of Pure Delight." He is speaking of a certain old hymn: "It has the gift to evoke the sound of voices we hear no longer, the touch of hands that are still. It recalls country churches and summer Sabbath mornings, men and women whose faces were grave and strong and dear; restless children (perhaps we were some of them); through open windows of plain glass the half-heard sound of horses shaking their harness and the gleam of marble or slate headstones beneath which the dead were at the rest they had so laboriously earned. . . ." An equally lovely passage breathing the same air of appreciation and leisure occurs in another of Dr. Atkins' sermons: "It [the music] filled the great concert chamber with tenderness and sudden brave resolutions and little sighing, singing

sounds which made friends with silence, and vibrant so-
norities which played a double music, once upon the key-
board and once upon the heartstrings. It filled the semi-
darkness not with sounds but with stars. . . ." It would
have been too bad not to have taken time for that.

Leisurely moments like these, even in a sermon that has-
tens to its end, open the window upon forgotten vistas or
unexplored realms of beauty or sentiment, and rest and
invigorate the souls of the listeners. If one is too much of
a poet he may be tempted to indulge this tendency where it
has no obvious place; as when one of our contemporary
preachers (one of the best of them) begins his sermon with
the words: "The Book of Ecclesiastes is on the face of it
a meditation of life from a vanished past of whose marble
and bronze little is left save broken columns which once lifted
sculptured gods and goddesses of heartbreaking beauty to
an azure sky."

This is lovely, to be sure. But it is too soon to be subjected
to any such feast of beauty, too much like beginning one's
dinner with dessert, or having roast turkey for breakfast.
Whether it conveys any perfectly clear meaning to the average hearer is doubtful. It is hardly a natural way of intro-
ducing the work of a " gentle cynic " like Ecclesiastes; and
it does not seem to put the speaker ahead in what he really
wants to say. But what I am after here is the fact that a
homiletic style can easily be too commonplace and too hur-
ried. Beauty and sentiment have a place in sermons as in
all good speaking or writing.

One matter already hinted at, in addition to the quickened
tempo of the modern sermon, is the modern preference for

the conversational rather than the more formal and oratorical style of earlier times. This also is to the good, since in conversation — if it is good conversation — we generally do say things with a minimum of waste and indirection. But public speech is not mere conversation. In almost every sermon, if not indeed in every one, there is a point — there may be many, but one is sure to come when the preacher sums up and drives home his thought in his concluding sentences — where the style ought to rise above the conversational level, and where if it does not do so you feel there is something lacking. When Lincoln said, in one of his addresses to Congress urging them to adopt a way out of slavery without war, "We shall nobly gain or meanly lose the last best hope of man," that was more than conversation, though every word in it is used in conversation every day. Cast the Gettysburg Address into conversational form and it not only ceases to be great literature, but it fails of the purpose for which it was given.

Eloquence, I suppose, is the fitting of style to matter; and there are matters that require not merely to be talked about but to be spoken of in words as dignified or as solemn or as beautiful as the things themselves. The man who has not mastered the conversational style lacks one of the sharpest tools of the public speaker. But the man who does not know when or how to rise out of it is little if anything more than a private talker who happens to be speaking in public. In the volume already referred to (*Pulpit Mirrors*) Dr. Byington expresses the conviction, born out of teaching many men to preach and out of listening to many preachers, that contemporary preaching could well stand a larger infusion of the oratorical element. He is quite right. There is so little oratory heard in the pulpit or anywhere else today that few men come to the ministry with any flair for it. But there is a place for oratory in the treatment of the great themes of religion. If when the preacher comes to this place he can only converse, he is almost as badly off as the preacher who wants to orate all the time.

There are some men, often very able and learned men, who apparently lack a natural feeling for language. They do not instinctively see why a thing should be said in one way rather than in another, nor why one way is so much better than another. They lack the instinct for saying things clearly, forcibly, picturesquely. Some learned and profound men have a genius for obscurity or indirection. In a volume by one of the greatest of contemporary American philosophers I find this sentence: "We keep our paths straight because we do not confuse the sequential, correlative and functional relationships of types of experience with the contemporaneous, correlative and structural distinctions of elements within a given function." Perhaps what the author wishes to say in this sentence cannot be said in any other way; as to this I have no means of judging, because I have no idea of what he intended to say. But if he had to say it this way he might as well not have said it at all. Indeed some learned men seem to have a genius even for bad grammar. One voluminous American writer seems generally to make his verb agree with the noun or nouns standing closest to it, irrespective of the subject of the verb. "Greek thought, from which stems the following conceptions," " the adjustment of means to ends are practical necessities," " the traits of a machine which marks its structure," may serve as examples. At this point I cannot avoid quoting a sentence from a history of religion in America — a fine history too —: "His education was received in a Jesuit school in Maryland and was later sent to St. Omer's College in France." It reminds one of the advertisement of the fruit company: " When thoroughly stewed even an invalid will enjoy our prunes." I do not quote these sentences to raise a laugh; they are truly melancholy. Much less do I quote them to show my disrespect for their writers; they are far more learned and able than I am. But that is just the point — some very able and learned men lack the natural feeling for language.

Not all the men who lack this feeling go into the ministry — the sentences I have just quoted were written by men outside it — but some of them do. For any man who has such a natural tendency toward entanglement in his speech, the current preference for the short sentence is a very present help in time of trouble. It is much easier to get twisted in a sentence of forty words than in one of ten. A man may lose his way in going from one end of the town to the other, but he can usually find it to the next corner. However, some deficiency in the feeling for language is apparently not only natural but inalienable to some men, and must just be put up with. In spoken discourse it is often corrected or at least concealed by the emphasis of the speaker, or is entirely outweighed by his evident earnestness and sincerity. Yet it must be confessed that a natural feeling for language is a great gift of God to the speaker. What he has to guard against is making language an end in itself; he should use language as the means of clarifying and enforcing the truth he has in mind.

The fundamental element in public speech is force. What the preacher is after is to get his ideas across to the people in front of him. And not merely across — not merely on the counter, so to speak, where people can see them and take them if they want to — but pushed upon them so that they are inescapable. Obviously what is required for this purpose is not primarily elegance or literary smoothness, but force. Any other element of style in spoken discourse is subordinate to that of force; every other element is valuable as it contributes to force.

How does one get force? Not by shouting, nor by lowering one's voice to a stage whisper, though an appropriate delivery may help much. Perhaps the first element in force, at least one of the most important, is clearness. Many years ago Herbert Spencer developed his " philosophy of style," based upon the principle of the economy of the reader's attention. The principle is even more important in spoken than in written discourse. Things that make an unnecessary draft upon the mental energy of the listener — like words that are unfamiliar to him, so that he has to stop and hunt their meaning while he loses the next few words, or involved sentences which make him stop and think about the words themselves — needlessly waste the attention of the hearer, deflect him from the main point, and diminish the force of what is said. When you are having a quarrel with a man you do not call him by any name that he does not instantly comprehend. I remember the instance of a cultivated but angry woman who called her neighbor a "virago." Since the neighbor had to wait till evening to ask her husband what virago meant, it may be inferred that the impression which the party of the first part wished to convey to the party of the second part was considerably weakened. I once asked one minister about the impression another had made on an occasion at which both had been present. "Oh," he said, "it was singularly infelicitous." The statement was excellent for the purpose intended, since the speaker, without using any such blunt and too easily understood words, wished to say that the man had made an ass of himself. But when a man wants force — not suggestiveness or implication, but force — let him use the shortest, commonest, most easily understood words he can command. Let him save his hearer's attention for the idea and not make him waste any of it upon the words. Simplicity, directness, clarity (they are the same thing) constitute force.

At this point the conversational style helps. When a man in one of my homiletics classes uses such words as "integrate," "rationalize," "coordinate," "depersonalize," "motivate," or other school-words, I ask him, "Would you say it to me personally in that way?" He says, "No, I wouldn't say, 'What motivated you to rationalize it in that manner'; I would say, 'Why did you give that excuse for it.'" In one of his essays which I read many years ago William Dean Howells says: "In an essay I write, 'I made the requisite purchases,' but in conversation I say, 'I bought what I needed.'" He argues that the latter style is better than the former even in an essay, since it says more simply and directly what the speaker has in mind. It is certainly better for a sermon. In an essay one can stop and ask what a phrase means; in a sermon, if he doesn't get the meaning as the speaker speaks he doesn't get it at all.

Brevity is another element in force. Here the conversational manner does not necessarily help, since in conversation we often use more words than are necessary. Yet this is not usually so in animated conversation. A rough but substantially accurate measure of force in style is the proportion of words to ideas. Whatever can be said in fifty words and is said in seventy-five is weakened by about fifty per cent. Nothing would be easier than to make the Lord's Prayer or the Twenty-third Psalm longer; such a procedure would also inevitably make them weaker. Bassanio said of Gratiano, "His reasons are as two grains of wheat hid in two bushels of chaff." The proportion is not right. Brevity is not the only virtue in the preacher, but it is a virtue which besides being good in itself greatly enhances any others he may have.

It is a significant remark of James Truslow Adams' concerning the two Gettysburg addresses made respectively by Edward Everett and President Lincoln, that one orator had spoken eight minutes and the other an hour and a quarter, and one of them had become immortal. The long speech could not have been made immortal by cutting it to eight minutes, but the short one could have been robbed of any hope of immortality by being strung out to an hour and a quarter.

Sometimes a man loses force and cumbers his style by an excessive desire for refinement of his meaning. This is often the reason for the insertion of qualifying phrases or the piling up of adjectives and adverbs. Some men seem to be always in a lexicographic frame of mind. It is not enough for them that you get their meaning; you must discriminate it from all other possible meanings. It is as if they could not say that the girl had on a red dress, but must specify the exact shade and explain how it differs from all other shades. There are doubtless times when such minute analysis is necessary, but as Jenkin Lloyd Jones used to say so wisely, "Analysis for the laboratory, synthesis for the pulpit." In a sermon, dealing as it usually does with some general moral or religious truth, which allows people to make their own qualifications, exceptions or abatements, and in which the speaker is supposed to be driving at a point, analysis is generally not only superfluous but weakening. It gives the impression that the speaker is more anxious to have his listeners discriminate between one thing and another on the way than he is to get them to their journey's end. A man may be a great preacher in spite of such a habit, but he would be a better one without it.

For example, in nineteen lines of a sermon by an eminent American preacher I counted twenty-seven adjectives and thirty-one nouns. But since some of these nouns did not admit of an adjective, others had two or three. On another page taken at random I found forty-nine adjectives and adverbs, on another thirty-eight. This habit of a too delicate refinement of ideas leads to the frequent use of adverbs to qualify adjectives — "simply absurd," "splendidly honest," "blindingly magnificent," "disconcertingly sincere," "rather desperate," "very singular," "rather startling," "sternly strong," "terribly final," "nobly authentic." I have said that such refinement produces delicate shades of meaning which probably cannot be had in any other way; but it also produces a style overburdened with fine distinctions, many of which will escape the ear of the listener and some of which do not need to be made. The general effect is to detract from the force of one's statements. To say that a thing is "rather terrible" is to reduce the terror of it; to say that something is "perfectly certain" is not to say anything more than that it is certain. If you can say that a thing is true you add nothing by saying that it is "absolutely true."

Most of the sayings that have stuck in the minds of men have few qualifying words in them. "Ye shall know the truth and the truth shall make you free": introduce a few adjectives or adverbs into this sentence and you have destroyed it. "Man is the measure of all things"; "Eat not thine heart"; "The soul is purified by terror and pity"; "Man shall not live by bread alone but by every word that proceedeth out of the mouth of Jehovah"; "In Him was life and the life was the light of men" — to qualify such statements is to weaken them. Jesus was a master of the art of stating things in the strongest possible way, letting people make their own qualifications and exceptions. He did not pare down the truth on both sides till there was nothing left of it. He said, "It is easier for a camel to go through the eye of a needle than for a rich man to enter the kingdom of God." He didn't specify how big a camel or how rich a man or what kind of needle. He said, "There is joy in heaven over one sinner that repenteth more than over ninety-and-nine just men who need no repentance" — and he did not add, "Though, to be sure, there is much to be said on the other side of this question, and I hope I shall not be misunderstood." He seemed to think that if he could get his main idea into people's minds they could shade it for themselves. Most of the sayings that have come down from long ago as part of our moral and spiritual inheritance are not dressed up; they come close to being naked truths. A man must write or speak as he must, and he may deliberately sacrifice the force of his utterance to the delicacy or refinement of it. But after all, force is the fundamental element in spoken discourse.

Other elements besides clarity, simplicity, brevity, and the use of familiar words help to make up force in speech. Beauty helps. In the instance I have already cited from Dr. Atkins — "tenderness and sudden brave resolutions and little sighing, singing sounds which made friends with silence" etc.— this little touch of beauty adds a force of its own. But it must always be a beauty that is called for in the place where it occurs. Beauty dragged in, leaning against the wall of the sermon like a pillar that supports nothing, is an excrescence. Sentiment also, if and where it belongs, is an element of force; let the same quotation from Dr. Atkins illustrate.

Picturesque or pictorial language is an element in force. It is sometimes said in a tone of reproach that most people think in pictures. So they do. So far as we think about things that can be put into pictures we always think in pictures whenever we think distinctly. It is doubtful whether anyone thinks in abstractions; certainly no one thinks in abstractions about ordinary and practical things such as go into sermons. When a man seems to be thinking in abstractions it is probable that he has thought so much about the thing he is discussing that what sound like abstractions to the rest of us are not such to him.

Anyway, there is force in concrete and pictorial talk. When Oliver Wendell Holmes says:

> They say that in his prime,
> Ere the pruning knife of time
> Cut him down,
> Not a better man was found
> By the crier on his round
> Through the town —

he talks in pictures. Everybody sees the pictures, therefore everybody gets the ideas. When Emilia discovers that her husband Iago has deceived Othello, and Desdemona piously says she hopes he may be pardoned, and Emilia answers, " A halter pardon him and hell gnaw his bones," she likewise talks in pictures. We always talk that way when we are aroused, because when we are aroused we talk forcibly. When old John Burns was accused by some of his labor associates of not having opposed a royal grant to the queen upon the birth of an heir to the throne, he did not reply in abstract terms about the sacredness of motherhood; he said, " I am the son of my mother and the husband of my wife. And if you ask me to put a public insult upon a woman who has just borne a child, I will not do it." That is talking in pictures. No other kind of talking is so forcible. Said Rufus Choate of an unseaworthy ship upon which many people had been drowned and whose survivors were now his clients, " She went down the harbor painted and perfidious, a coffin but no ship." But I need not labor this point, nor give further illustration of it. I suppose everybody admits it, though not all preachers remember it. Most preachers who have outgrown the fear of being called morons because they talk in pictures, and who have been out of school long enough to have learned how to do so, talk in pictures as much as they can.

I have referred incidentally to the use of the short and familiar word in preference to the long and unfamiliar one. Listeners will have their preferences about this, and speakers will have their habits. But most listeners will grasp ideas more easily if they are couched in the language which they themselves habitually use. Any preacher who cares to do so can easily cultivate the " Anglo-Saxon " style, as it is called. There is a good deal of nonsense talked about vocabulary. Some preachers, mostly young ones, are ambitious to acquire a larger and more erudite stock of words. The effort to do so is misplaced. Especially in oral speech, apart from technical terms, the words in common use are generally the best, and no words which one has to acquire consciously will do him any service. An unusually large vocabulary is no better for the average man than an unusually large hat. Where an unusual vocabulary fits, as in the case of Carlyle, it is because the man and his thought are unusual. A unique vocabulary sought for its own sake is like a shadow with nothing to cast it. A larger vocabulary, except as it is demanded and created by a larger thought, is only a suit of clothes much too big. Since we think in words, when a man gets an idea he will get the words with which to express it. The idea comes clothed in words; to express it in words other or more unusual than those it naturally comes in is merely to disguise it.

It is possible to use language that sounds lovely and means nothing. The best illustration of this that I have observed comes, happily, from outside the pulpit. It occurs in Mark Twain's "Double Barreled Detective Story." "It was a crisp and spicy morning in early October," says Mark. " The lilacs and the laburnums, lit with the glory fires of Autumn, hung burning and flashing in the upper air, a fairy bridge provided by kind nature for the wingless wild things that have their home in the tree tops and would visit together. The larch and pomegranate flung their purple flames along the slanting sweep of woodland. The sensuous fragrance of innumerable deciduous flowers rose upon the swooning atmosphere. Far in the empty sky a solitary oesophagus slept upon motionless wing. Everywhere brooded stillness, serenity and the peace of God." A teacher in the Philippine Islands wrote Mark that he had been reading this passage and had been much impressed with its beauty until he came upon the word " oesophagus," which gave him pause. Commenting upon the passage and the letter of the teacher Mark says: " Nothing in the paragraph disturbed him but that one word. It shows that the paragraph was most ably constructed for the deception it was intended to put upon the reader. It was my intention that it should read plausibly, and it is now plain that it does. Alas, if I had but left that one treacherous word out I should have scored, scored everywhere, and the paragraph would have slid through every reader's sensibilities, like oil, and left not a suspicion behind. . . . I told him to read carefully the whole paragraph and he would find not a vestige of sense in any detail of it." I quote this passage and the comments upon it not because the preacher is tempted to play any such joke upon his congregation, but because he may unconsciously be betrayed into something of the same sort on a less pretentious scale. The point I wish to make here is that he could not easily do so, or would surely catch himself, if he spoke in words of one syllable such as are used around the house. Their meaning is too plain both to himself and to his hearers.

It may be nothing but a personal prejudice, or it may be only because I have never been able to acquire a multifarious and variegated vocabulary; but I seem to myself to prefer the Anglo-Saxon vocabulary because it lends itself to simplicity, clearness, definiteness, and thus to the fundamental element in all spoken style — force. If one uses such a vocabulary he must be prepared to be thought shallow and superficial in comparison with the user of longer words less easily understood. He may be able to live down this adverse judgment, or he may not. Most people will continue to think that ideas which they take in easily are superficial while those they do not grasp are deep and profound. If one must suffer this adverse judgment for the cause even to the end, it is a mild sort of martyrdom and worth suffering. At any rate, I come back to my statement that force is the fundamental element in pulpit style, and that everything else is to be judged by whether it adds to or detracts from this.

Perhaps a fair description of a good pulpit style is that it be such that people will understand what the preacher means and be able, if they want, to remember it till the next day. Yet that is not quite enough. It should be such that people cannot easily escape the preacher's meaning, nor quickly and easily let it go. If it be asked whether a preacher's style may not be too good, the answer depends upon what you mean by good. It can be too ornate, too beautiful; because wherever you have beauty that is not called for you have an excrescence, even if it is a pretty one. If the style suggests that the preacher is more intent upon it than upon his thought, and depends upon it rather than upon his ideas to make his impression, you get the feeling that he is too much of an actor — the feeling, not that he has convictions which he is struggling to utter as best he can, since the convictions mean much more to him than the mode of their utterance; it is rather as if he had got hold of some ideas which will do well enough for his purpose — other ideas would do if he didn't happen to have got hold of these — his purpose being to show what he can do with them. It is not thus that men speak who are deeply impressed with the truth of what they say and with its importance for human life.

I do not mean to imply that there are many preachers who give one this impression; but it is an impression that can be produced by a certain kind of preaching; and it is pretty nearly always produced where the preacher is primarily a word artist whose ideas are only canvas or colors to him. From the editor's introductions to individual sermons in a volume of collected sermons I quote a few sentences which will illustrate my point.

Of one sermon the editor says: " Withal it is so wise, so finely poised, so aglow with confident expectation, as befits those who would follow One who 'made as though he would have gone further' on a sacramental eventide." Of another he declares: " It reveals much of the same artistry of insight, imagery and rhythm; and it must surely find response in those who feel the pathos and passion and prophecy of the modern yearning for spiritual reality." Of another he says that its author's ministry was " a triumph from the beginning — best of all, for its suggestion of a ' drift of pinions ' which ' would we harken, beats on our clay-shuttered doors.' " Of a fourth: " In the sermon following we see a noble intelligence moving in a large orbit, making the august reality of an Unseen order real, commanding, and consecrating." He speaks of the author of still another of the sermons as being " a poet, a mystic, a seerlike mind, its visions and visitations, its moods and memories, recalled in mellow, meditative years, in a style limpid and lovely — like an old violin which remembers all the melodies it has heard."

I should be sorry to seem to speak unappreciatively of such words of introduction; but one can hardly fail to ask, Was it this way that anyone would naturally have spoken who had listened to Jeremiah or Amos, or who had even read the words of these men out of a book two thousand years later? Isn't there just a hint that what the editor is looking for in the sermons he has collected is some sort of prettiness? The preacher is an artist, and he need never fear that he will be too good an artist; but he is an artist who deals in ideas, not in words, and when the words get to be anything more than the vehicle for the ideas they are a sort of intoxicant or soporific.

One may get help on the acquisition of a good literary

style from books that have been written for the purpose. One of the best I have seen recently is *Inductive English Composition,* by Starbuck and Raymond, two English teachers in the University of Iowa. In addition to a minute and careful study of paragraphs, sentences and words, it has an abundance of well selected prose from all periods of English and American literature. But the minister cannot go back to study this or any other such book. What it can do for him should have been done in college. Yet many men have come out of college without its having been done for them. They get a little help perhaps from their homiletics courses in theological school, but the professor of homiletics is not a teacher of English. And too many preachers get through both college and seminary and into the ministry without having acquired a reasonably good style.

If the preacher is unconscious of defects in this matter and satisfied with what he is doing, nothing can help him. If he recognizes his deficiency and would like to improve himself, the best rule he can follow is to read widely, and the best books. The acquirement of style is largely an unconscious process. If a man who has some appreciation of music, but no technical training in it, will just listen to as much music as he has time for, doing his best to discriminate between what is better and what is not so good, he will finally come to enjoy good music — at least as good music as the Lord intended him to enjoy. Most of us know little about pictures and have few if any means of getting a technical appreciation or understanding of them. If we never see any but a few pictures, mostly of an ordinary sort, we remain in this matter about where we started. But if for any reason we have occasion to wander through many art galleries, looking and admiring, approving or disapproving, we finally come to know a good picture from a bad one.

The matter of style is somewhat the same — but with a difference. The man who knows good music may not be able to produce music either good or bad; one may recognize a good picture without attempting to paint. But it is the business of the preacher to write and speak. In some fashion, better or worse, he is already doing this. Being thus already started at this craft, he writes better as he comes to admire and appreciate good literature. He may improve his taste in pictures without learning how to handle a brush, or in music without acquiring any skill of his own at the piano. But he cannot acquire a good taste in literature without himself writing and speaking more effectively.

It is true that some literary men have put themselves through a rigid discipline in the acquisition of style. Stevenson practiced writing in the manner of Defoe, then of Burke, and so on. This practice served to put him on more intimate terms with the different styles of the men whom he took as models, as well as to sharpen his sense of beauty and power in speech. When Rudyard Kipling brought suit against an American firm for a violation of his copyright he alleged, as part of his ground for action, that it had taken him twenty years to develop his own peculiar style. Though such methods as these would doubtless make the preacher's sense of style more acute and give him flexibility and facility in the use of language, they are too laborious for the average man; nor has he time for them. He will accomplish the same end in a smaller but sufficient way through the unconscious influence upon him of the authors he reads. Let him read, if he wishes to, with the idea in mind that he also is a producer of literature and has a style to attain. But much better, let him read for the sake of appreciation and enjoyment, for this is one of the places — and there are many such — where we learn more if we are not too conscious of learning.

Yet the preacher does not write like an essayist, or a novelist, or like anyone but a preacher. Whatever he admires in other writers, let him remember what kind of style he wants for himself. Terse, concentrated, with a minimum of words to ideas, simple, picturesque, clear, forcible — that is the kind of style he wants. Reading good literature will cure him of setting up false standards and give a certain elevation to his style, but it will not necessarily leave him with a style that is good for the pulpit. For the special traits that distinguish good spoken discourse from a style that might be good for novels or essays or anything else, he must just watch himself. If a man comes out of the theological school with a habit of genuine and severe self-criticism, it will be worth more to him than anything else he has learned there. But if he hasn't got it there, he can get it afterwards.

Yet here again, as I have said before, the greatest help to a better, more simple, direct, and forcible style, comes from a man's interest in what he is saying. Let him believe in that; let it be something that commands the whole assent of his judgment and his feelings, and he will not be content to say it in any way but his best. If the preacher has the right kind of material and any natural literary gift, what he says will almost of itself command the right kind of style.

I cannot insist upon this too often. A mere preoccupation with style will often defeat its own end. Let the thing with which the preacher deals engross him wholly, and his style will follow the lead. There is a passage, I think in the *Phaedo,* where Socrates convicts one of his interlocutors of saying something that has no sense. Jowett translates his recantation in the words, "I inadvertently spoke nonsense." But the literal translation of what he said is, "I escaped myself, saying nothing." He said nothing, and didn't know it. When the preacher does the same, he can't expect to say it, whatever it is, very well.

The preacher will naturally be a reader of contemporary literature. Some of this may not be so good as the best literature of the same kind out of the past, but he will want to read it because it is what his contemporaries are saying. The greatest single literary vehicle these days is the novel. On the whole the novelists probably exercise more control over popular thought than any other writers. They make their novels the medium of their ideas upon social, political, and economic matters, and especially of their underlying philosophy of morals. If this philosophy is not always what we approve, it is what our people read and absorb. What people read in their leisure hours, without any intention of being affected, generally affects them most. In all our parishes there are people whose ideas go back not to anything they learned in school, but to Galsworthy, Wells, Hemingway, Huxley, Edith Wharton, Rebecca West, Sinclair Lewis, Somerset Maugham, Thomas Mann. The preacher who has to snatch time for the reading of fiction will often wish that some of this modern fiction were not so terribly long.

He may also regret that some of it is so unnecessarily nasty. He may prefer (as I often do) to read something he already knows is good rather than something else just to find out whether it is good or not. I know that *Vanity Fair* and *Pickwick* are good, but to read them again does not do for me what reading *Anthony Adverse* or *Gone With the Wind* does. To be a man of his own generation one must know what his contemporaries are saying. If he gets nothing else out of modern fiction, he gets an index to the current popular taste.

He will get much besides this, of course — many suggestions for sermon topics, much illustrative material. To refer in one's sermon to some striking scene in a novel which he knows half his congregation is reading establishes an intimate contact between speaker and listeners. Their published sermons show how often and effectively many preachers do this. If I say nothing more about current fiction it is because my readers are doubtless as familiar with it as I am — many of them more so.

There is one other contemporary literary movement which it will pay the preacher to know intimately. That is the modern poetry movement. He may go back to Emily Dickinson and Walt Whitman, the forerunners of the movement in America, or he may confine himself to the output of the last generation. If modern poetry is a new field for him, or if he knows only here and there a contemporary poet and wishes to have a more inclusive view, let him take either of two volumes published at a time when the new poetry movement was most self-conscious: Marguerite Wilkinson's *New Voices* or Harriet Monroe's *The New Poetry*. In either of these books he will find a comprehensive account of the movement — who the " new " poets are and how they differ from the old; how they treat nature, love, religion, and the perennial themes of the poets. In *New Voices* he will find special treatment of such items as diction, rhythm, symbols, images, and some two hundred poems quoted by way of illustration.

By the time he has read this volume, especially if he will add to it Harriet Monroe's *The New Poetry,* with its poems from a hundred representatives of the new movement, its critical comments upon their work, and its bibliography of twenty pages, he will be convinced — if he has been in doubt about it — that there exists a new era in American poetry of such extent and significance that it would be a great mistake for him to be ignorant of it.

He may still further introduce this movement to himself through Alfred Kreymborg's *Our Singing Strength* or Louis Untermeyer's *The New Era in American Poetry.* In these works he will make the acquaintance of practically all the best representatives of the new movement. This acquaintance he will wish to deepen and extend in the case of certain of the more outstanding poets. He will probably want to read Edgar Lee Masters' *Spoon River Anthology;* Carl Sandburg's *Chicago Poems,* and perhaps his latest volume, *The People, Yes;* William Rose Benét's *John Brown's Body,* and a volume each of Robert Frost, E. A. Robinson, and Vachel Lindsay.

But for the most part the best of the modern poets are to be found in anthologies. One of the most comprehensive of these is Kreymborg's *Lyric America,* which contains a list of two hundred books of poetry including thirty-five other anthologies. More usable perhaps are the smaller volumes compiled by Jessie Rittenhouse, *The Little Book of Modern Verse, Second Little Book of Modern Verse,* and several others which she has since added to these. In the work of the great poets of the past, like Tennyson, Browning, and Wordsworth, there is a vast amount that will not live. It is a great convenience to have the best of what they have done gathered into a single volume, like Matthew Arnold's edition of Wordsworth's shorter poems. There are also in every generation men and women who do not produce a large body of poetry but do write a few things that rank with the best. So of these contemporary poets. If one has a few of the best things that any of them have produced, including those who have not written voluminously but have written well, he has what he needs. Anthologies duplicate one another over large sections, so that it is no advantage to have too many of them.

On the whole I should say that any one of the introductions I have mentioned, covering the whole new poetry movement in a comprehensive, critical and explanatory way; a volume each of Robert Frost, Carl Sandburg, E. A. Robinson and William Rose Benét; and three or four good anthologies, will make a library on the subject that will be wholly adequate for one's needs. One would have to invest in this library not more than what a new suit of clothes would cost him (I am assuming that he wears ready-made clothes and not too good ones), and if he can make the old suit do a little longer I should say the library investment would be a good one.

In the new poetry he will find some things that astonish him, and some over which he will hardly know whether to smile or to feel sad. It has its " lunatic fringe " as most such new movements have. When he reads Miss Marianne Moore's poem " The Labors of Hercules " he may at least see in it the depths of obscurity which can be achieved even in poetry. But he will find Sara Teasdale's little poem, " Let It Be Forgotten," as lovely as anything Tennyson ever wrote. For the candid expression of doubt in religion he will appreciate Anna Hempstead Branch's " An Unbeliever." In James Stephens' " What Thomas an Buile Said in a Pub " he will find a somewhat bizarre but altogether lovely treatment of the human conception of God.

I have briefly remarked elsewhere upon the use of poetry in sermons. A too free employment of it is certainly not wise, but if a man must quote poetry, modern poetry generally has the advantage of being brief, as well as representative of the thought and feeling of our own time. Even if one never quotes poetry, what the poets think about life in general and about religion in particular is certainly important; and I would recommend a study of this new poetry not merely for occasional quotation from the pulpit, but much more for its stimulus to the preacher, its brevity and picturesqueness, and the additional insight it will give him into the thought of his own times.

There is one influence which the reading of poetry, of whatever age, should have upon the style of the preacher. All good poetry is sensuous and concrete. It never deals with abstractions; it talks in figures, images and symbols; it does not argue; it does not draw morals; it paints the idea in pictures; it doesn't "exhaust the subject," but puts it before the reader in a few bold strokes; it lets the truth it expresses make its own appeal; it assumes that the reader will also have some imagination, and allows him to use it.

All these are characteristics which the preacher, in his own way and in accordance with the purpose of his speaking, ought also to have. To gain these qualities in his manner of speaking, it is not necessary that the poetry he reads be "new" poetry. When I have had in my class some man whose tendency was to talk in school-words and drown his hearers in abstractions, I have often advised him that when he sits down to write his sermon he first read a scene out of *Hamlet* or *King Lear*. He may even need to pause in the middle of his writing and read it again. This practice is a sure cure, or as sure as any there is, for the disease of abstractness.

The reading of poetry should have still another effect upon the preacher's style. The poets use simple language and short words. In the quotation from "The Last Leaf" on page 80 there are thirty words. Out of the thirty there are only three which have two syllables, and these are such simple and familiar words as "better," "crier," and "pruning." In the little speech of Hamlet to Horatio near the end of the play —

> If thou didst ever hold me in thine heart,
> Absent thee from felicity awhile,
> And in this harsh world draw thy breath in pain
> To tell my story —

there are twenty-seven words. "Absent," "awhile," and "story" have two syllables each, "felicity" four; the rest of the words have one syllable. To be sure, Shakespeare can also say, " the multitudinous seas incarnadine," and he never gives the impression of avoiding a word because it is unusual. The peculiar stage of development which the language had reached in his time, and Shakespeare's own genius, gave him a vocabulary unrivaled among English poets. The wonder is that with such a wealth of the means of expression in his hands he still remains such a master of perfectly simple speech and still uses that for the utterance of his deepest emotions.

> For God's sake, let us sit upon the ground
> And tell sad stories of the death of kings;

> If you can look into the seeds of time,
> And say which grain will grow and which will not —

in such passages the preacher finds a model of simple English style fit for spoken discourse.

It is the same with other poets. Take Shelley's little " Indian Serenade," of which the first stanza runs:

> I arise from dreams of thee
> In the first sweet sleep of night,
> When the winds are breathing low
> And the stars are shining bright.
> I arise from dreams of thee,
> And a spirit in my feet
> Hath led me — who knows how?
> To thy chamber window, sweet —

or Stevenson's " Requiem,"

> Under the wide and starry sky
> Dig the grave and let me lie;

> Glad did I live and gladly die,
> And I laid me down with a will —

or Kipling's

> When 'Omer smote 'is bloomin' lyre
> He'd heard men sing by land and sea,
> And what he thought he might require,
> He went and took, the same as me —

and you will have an idea of the simple, sensuous kind of language which the poet always uses and on which the preacher may well model his own style. I do not mean to say that poets always use words of one syllable, but as I once heard Dr. Coffin say, no word should go into a public prayer which would be out of place in a lyric poem. This rule does not hold quite so strictly for a sermon as for a prayer, and yet I think — and this is what I am driving at — that nothing can be better for the style of the preacher than a perfect familiarity with English poetry. It is better if one gains this familiarity during the period when his habits of self-expression are still forming; indeed that is the natural time for the reading of much poetry — in the period of adolescence while one's emotions are yeasty and he is feeling about for sentiments and for self-expression. But if one has not got it then, he can get this familiarity with poetry at any time he will. I recall that Samuel Gompers acquired a reading knowledge of German for the sake of reading the labor literature printed in that language and not translated. If an unschooled man would put himself to such a discipline at a mature age for such a purpose, it is not too much for a preacher to make the acquaintance of any kind of literature that will make him a better preacher.

Chapter Five

PREPARATION OF THE SERMON

I N MANY instances the best sermons are those that require and receive the least preparation; they just grow. If sermons grew every week there would be no occasion to say anything about their preparation. But they do not; they come once in a while, to the preacher's delight and surprise, and are generally the result of much reading, brooding, and experience, perhaps forgotten by the preacher himself. The theory of the subconscious mind would suffice to explain them. Only we do not seem to know so much about the subconscious mind as we did some years ago. And if it were all that, a few years ago, it was said to be, it ought to produce more sermons, as well as more of everything else, than it does.

But what is clear to everybody from his own experience is that the contents of the mind are not all upon its surface. Things appear in the mind and disappear from it, yet seem still to be somewhere in it. And sometimes they come to the surface again in a more developed form than that in which we remember having last seen them. If this statement sounds too much as if the mind were a place — like a box, or a house with several stories and a basement — where things go on which the mind knows nothing about, perhaps we could put it in another way and say that the mind works on certain things and then lays them aside, works on them again and lays them aside, till finally, when it calls them up to work on them yet again, they seem to be all done. This statement would seem to imply either that the mind while it had these matters before it had done more upon them than it was aware of, or else that it went on working on them after it thought it had dismissed them. Since neither of these statements sounds very sensible, perhaps I had better forsake the role of amateur psychologist and merely say that in some manner we do not wholly understand, upon occasion and to some extent, ideas have a way of developing themselves and thoughts a way of arranging themselves apart from our conscious and intentional occupation with them. So it comes that at times even a sermon seems to spring full-born from the head of the preacher.

In earlier times the appearance of such a sermon would have been attributed to inspiration; but nobody believes in inspiration in the old sense any more, though many preachers waste a good deal of time waiting for one. "Hunches," if not inspiration, do come to one now and then. There are times when thinking or writing, whether a sermon or anything else, seems the easiest thing in the world to do, seems almost to do itself. There are other times — and alas, they come oftener and last longer — when to put ideas together and give them significant form seems like labor for which the human being was not intended. But Sunday is coming, as the preacher knows only too well, and when it comes he must have for his people something not wholly unworthy of them or of himself and his high calling.

The people actually pay him for talking to them. That is a sobering thought, sometimes even a saddening one. They not only pay him the compliment of sitting still for thirty minutes while he talks to them — which in itself is a great deal — but in addition to that they actually pay him for talking. If he did not follow a high and holy calling, if there were no other considerations than the somewhat worldly ones just adduced, he must have something worth listening to to say on Sunday. If one of his inspirations would come, how convenient that would be. But the subconscious mind seems to be on a sit-down strike, and there is no telling when it will go to work again — probably not this week; maybe not for the next six months; maybe never again. He hesitates to abandon himself to a prospect so dire as this last. No, inspiration will come again. But when? The preacher cannot wait for it — that's flat.

That being the case there is nothing for him to do but to go to work and produce. Produce, produce, produce — that's what he has to do, one week after another, for years on end — produce. No wonder the prospect frightens some young preachers. Perhaps — I am not sure — there are some entirely able men who are not equal to the task of production. They have acquisitive minds and can take in no end of what other men have done; they have critical minds and can evaluate what other men have produced, sometimes more accurately than the men who have produced it; they have analytical minds and can take apart what other men have put together, put their fingers on its strength and weakness more surely than the men who created it. But to produce, regularly and constantly, and stuff of a reasonably good kind, is not easy for them, perhaps not in them.

As I said, I am not sure this is true. Perhaps any reasonably bright man can learn to produce. But certainly no man in the ministry can excuse himself for not producing by saying, " I have a critical mind," or " I have an analytical mind." If a man hires out to be a painter he must paint, and not merely criticize or evaluate what someone else has painted. The minister is in a calling where he has placed himself under obligation to produce.

One other thing is clear at this point: the critical mood and the creative mood are at odds. One cannot exercise them, at least not equally, at the same time. When the time for production comes it is time to put the critical mood aside. I have known a man, an uncommonly able man, who never seemed able to divorce his critical from his creative faculties. He would write one page of a sermon and stop to read it over. It never seemed to him as good as it ought to be, nor as good as he knew he could make it; so he would tear it up and write a new page. He would repeat this performance all forenoon, and lunch time found him still on the first page. He never did learn how to produce, and finally fell into the habit of going into the pulpit and there producing on the spur of the moment. Except very incidentally, the time for criticism is after production. Let a man say to himself while he is writing, " I know this is not as good as it ought to be, but I must get ahead." Let him get ahead till he gets to the end, then take what he has written and criticize it as severely as he will. Let him rewrite page after page, or the whole thing, if he will. If he has time for such a system his product will be greatly improved. If he does not have time for it, or has time for only part of it, he has at least produced something.

Let the world turn round; Sunday can't catch him in complete undress.

I venture to speak of this matter, obvious as it is, because I once wasted hours in the way I have described. I would sometimes get a sermon half written, then conclude that the subject was wrong and that I never could make anything out of it, throw it away, and begin on something new. I had to cure myself of such habits by main force. I learned after a while that one's critical faculty, not wholly reliable at any time, is least so while one is in the throes of production. While he is writing it one does not always know either how good or how bad what he is writing is, nor how it will look as a part of the sermon when the whole has been completed.

The habit of self-criticism is invaluable, and no man will ever improve without it. It is to be exercised upon every sermon so far as time will allow. I have known a few men — Dr. Washington Gladden was one — who when they had once composed a sermon changed scarcely a word of it before preaching it. But I am not sure that they did not miss a great opportunity. It certainly will not do for the ordinary preacher to assume that what he has done at the first stroke is the best he can do. It seldom is; why indeed should it be? For myself I confess that the best work I do on any sermon is done in the two or three hours spent in making revisions after my first draft has been run through the typewriter. When I have the typewritten sermon before me I can see it. I can stand off and look at it almost as if someone else had written it. I can see what has crept in that doesn't need to be there, and I can take it out. I can see how one point does not follow so obviously from another, as I thought it did while I was writing. Sometimes I can see that certain items should be rearranged and that what I have said on page nine belongs on page three, or vice versa. I can break up a long sentence produced under my own momentum, and substitute a series of telling strokes in place of a continuous, uniform pressure. I can substitute a colorful word for a drab one, a picturesque phrase for a dull one. But most of all I can cut out unnecessary words or sentences, occasionally even a paragraph. Restraint has been said to be the secret of good writing — an incomplete recipe, I think, since there must be something to restrain before you can better it by restraining it. You can make a good penman out of a boy who writes a big, loose, flowing, generous hand, but hardly out of one who writes a cramped, crabbed one. While in the heat of production most of us write more profusely than we can afterwards justify. That is fortunate, for profuseness makes it unnecessary to add much upon revision. It gives one a chance to lop off excrescences, avoid repetitions, and cut down redundancies. To write as expansively as one wants to while he is in the process of composition gives one material upon which to exercise restraint when he looks through his work to see where restraint would improve it. But this is to be done afterwards, after the sermon has been written and one can take a good look at it. To exercise restraint while writing is to keep oneself at a perpetual walk, never permitting the exhilaration of a good gallop.

I have spoken as if all sermons should be written. Is that necessary? Of course not. And yet, unless a man has exceptional gifts as a speaker, unless he is better able than are most of us to keep both his thought and his style in mind without writing, there are advantages in writing which cannot be had in any other way. What a man is to do with his manuscript after he has written it is another matter. But probably no man, certainly very few men, can say something of twenty-five or thirty minutes' length so logically, compactly or forcibly the first time as the second or third time. To write, and read over, and correct, and rewrite, is to have said something two or three times before one says it in the pulpit.

Even if the preacher never uses his manuscript in the pulpit, the greater condensation, clarity and picturesqueness gained through writing will react upon his extemporaneous speech. Since, in saying any given thing, one will almost always use more words than upon later scrutiny appear necessary, I do not see how the preacher who never writes can quite avoid an inaccuracy, an inelegance, and especially a looseness and prolixity of which careful writing would be almost sure to cure him. I gladly admit that there are men who can accomplish without writing what the rest of us can do only with it. I read with amazement, almost with incredulity, the statement of Van Wyck Brooks that the historian Prescott was able to " compose in his memory to such an extent that he could often carry in his mind as many as three chapters of one of his books, seventy-two pages of printed text." But Prescott was a genius, and he was blind. Let blind geniuses follow his example. For those of us who have any native prolixity, looseness or illogicality, and no miraculous memory, writing is almost, if not quite, a necessity. It has this advantage, not to be despised, that it insures that no sermon will be produced without a minimum of work, the work necessary to write it through; and that is probably more work than many sermons get.

Still on this matter of writing — a study of writers who have attained any great distinction will show that most of them wrote and corrected and rewrote again and again. Stevenson did so; and it is almost too evident that Ruskin did so, for his style is almost too perfect and everywhere glorious. A fine piece of testimony comes from Dr. William E. Dodd, professor of history in the University of Chicago and recently American ambassador to Berlin. Dr. Dodd says: " This business of writing . . . is one of the most difficult things in the world. . . . As to my own writing, some of your students may be encouraged perhaps when I say that everything I put out has been written from three to five times. Yet rarely do I see a printed page of mine which does not seem in some sense inadequate to the purpose I had in mind, namely of expressing the exact truth in the clearest language." The preacher can hardly write every sermon three or four times, but that is all the more reason he should write it once. One of our popular magazines has a custom of printing at the head of each article, " Reading time sixteen minutes," " Reading time eighteen minutes," etc. A correspondent recently wrote to this magazine, " Shouldn't this be 'writing time'?" One feels that way about some sermons.

I recur to the question, How does one produce? First of all, he sits down and thinks. So far as I know, there is no particular way to think. We just naturally think when we are face to face with anything that makes us do so. If one is driving along a country road and comes to the end of it, he thinks about what to do next; he thinks till he finds out. But what is it he does when he thinks? About all that can be said is that ideas of what to do arise in his mind. For obvious reasons he rejects one idea, and another rises in its place. He tries that out, either in imagination or in actual practice, and if it does not work he finds another idea rising in his mind and ready to be tried. In such a case it is no effort to think; one does not force himself to think, the situation keeps him at it. All he can do, apparently, is to test or try out one idea after another as they rise in his mind; he cannot compel them to rise there.

What a man does when he produces a sermon is like this, with a difference. His subject does not compel him to think, as the unexpected end of the road does. He cannot let his mind wander from the end of the road, and he doesn't have to call it back, because the situation puts him in a dilemma from which he wants to escape. The subject of a sermon has presumably no such compelling power over the preacher. He can think about it, or on the other hand he can think about something else if he prefers. But he is aware that he is thinking about the sermon, and as often as he finds himself thinking about something else he can call his attention back to his sermon. This seems to be all he can do by way of forcing his ideas on the subject. So long as he keeps his subject in mind, ideas will arise concerning it. What sort of ideas will depend upon what sort of mind he has, how much he knows, whether his imagination is alive, and so on. But he cannot create ideas about the subject, and he does not need to. If he will keep his mind on it, all the ideas he has or is capable of having at the moment will rise to the surface. The mind is a thinking machine. It is always throwing up ideas, of one sort or another, about one subject or another. All a man can do about it is to see that it throws up ideas on one subject rather than on another. He can then select from among these ideas, and arrange them to suit his purpose.

Some of the ideas that rise in his mind will be usable just as they come. Others will be unusable, irrelevant, inappropriate, even mistaken. One idea sends him to a book, another he has not time to follow to the end or judge properly at the moment. But the book to which he goes and the idea that he follows further both keep his attention on his subject. However, in order to produce what he can produce, all he can do is to sit down before the subject, look at it, turn it around and examine it from every possible angle, ask questions about it, handle it, deal with it any way he can. Some such method is his only clue.

This is why, about those things concerning which we have already thought a good deal, a sermon, or the material for it, soon emerges. It is also why every preacher should get the subject of his sermon in mind as long beforehand as he can. It takes time for ideas to rise; it takes longer to judge them, sort them out, reject some, accept others, and bring them into proper arrangement. All this must come before the writing. If the subject is a fruitful and suggestive one, or the preacher in a peculiarly productive mood, it can be done in an hour, or in a few hours at the most. But the minister has many things to do besides composing his sermon. Funerals, weddings, pastoral calls, committee meetings and a hundred other things call his attention elsewhere. If he has his subject in mind early enough, so that in spite of such interruptions all the ideas he is capable of producing will have had time to rise to the surface, then in spite of the interruptions he will produce something worth preaching. If he is already fairly well started in this process even interruptions do not wholly stop him. On the way to the committee meeting or on the way home from the funeral, his mind recurs to his subject and the work of production goes on. The poor quality of some of the sermons produced by men who are capable of producing good sermons is due to the fact that this process of attention, thinking, brooding, incubation, has been begun too late and has therefore been too brief, and ideas worthy of the man or the subject have not had time to rise or to be properly worked over.

This is the reason why the preacher should not spend the whole week up to Saturday merely picking out his subject. Most of us at some period of our ministerial lives have wasted a good deal of time in that way. I used to have in mind three or four topics on which to preach on Sunday. I would stand off and look at them, and now one of them would look good to me, now another, and sometimes all of them would look bad. I would look at one of them and say, " It doesn't appeal to me "; at another and say, " It doesn't open up." I didn't seem to realize that if, when I was presumably in my right mind, I had thought these subjects good, then they probably were good; nor that it was now time for me to take one of them and open it up myself instead of waiting for it to open up to me — as if it were a poppy or an insurance agent. A man may have three or four topics in mind that he has long thought he would preach about — say, at random, "Hunger and Love," "The Homely Virtues," "Conflict and Cooperation," "God in Our Everyday Life." As he glances at these somewhere along the first of the week none of them looks very inviting. Yet all of them come close to life, individual or social; all of them have to do with religion; there is enough to be said about any one of them. He may spend all the week till Saturday afternoon in deciding between them, or falling back upon his earlier judgment that any one of them would make a good sermon he can pounce upon one of them and begin. I say, let him pounce. Life is short; Sunday comes quickly. All time spent deciding between topics equally good is wasted.

Every man will find such aids in his production as will really help him. Some men will work far ahead of time. I once knew a Methodist minister who had a whole year's sermons written in advance. Each week he wrote a new one to be preached a year from then. What he did when something occurred in the parish to render inappropriate the sermon intended for that Sunday, or when something happened in the country which he had not foreseen and which needed attention from the pulpit, he did not tell me. When this man told me about this habit of his (for his case is not apocryphal however impossible it may sound) I was much impressed with it as compared to my own less forehanded methods, and I resolved to do better. But he also told me that he once had a funeral sermon all written for a member of his congregation who had gone away to die, as everybody expected. But he didn't die; he got well, came home, and ultimately outlived his pastor. This story gave me pause. I perceived that the race is not always to the swift, and I resolved not to emulate this man too closely. I once got two weeks ahead in my sermon preparation, but the next week I was too busy to write a sermon.

In fact, most of us probably work better under a reasonable pressure. How can one get up steam when he knows that if he doesn't arrive this week it will be all right? I don't have to know what I shall preach about on the third Sunday of next month, but I do know that I must have a sermon ready for next Sunday. Within each week, when it is time to get at it, I want to know as early as possible what I am to do. I want time enough, but I don't want all the time in the world; I do better if I don't have so much time.

In the preparation of sermons preachers have used all sorts of devices for having material on hand when they need it. Clipping and filing systems, for instance. I have tried all that I have heard of. I never got any help from any of them, though I know many preachers who say they could not live without them. I read with my pencil in hand. When I get through with a book I usually know how to find in it anything that has struck me as having any particular value for me. If an idea that I want occurs to me later on, when I am writing a sermon, I can easily find it. If it does not occur to me I conclude that I do not need it.

I also have a looseleaf notebook in which I jot down subjects or minor items that occur to me while I am reading. I look through this frequently, sometimes adding something to a notation I have already made. Even this notebook is not such a mine as I thought it would be, or as I wish it were. I often find there something that I can use; but quite as often I ask myself, "Why did I ever write that down?" I say this not in depreciation of more methodical and forehanded men, but for the comfort of those who may be somewhat like me in this respect, to assure them that it isn't fatal, at any rate. But in such matters, every man to his own way.

I have spoken thus far of the preparation of the sermon, meaning thereby the immediate preparation. There is another kind of preparation, not for any one particular sermon but for any number of sermons. This preparation, without which no immediate preparation will produce much, consists in the reading and study I have spoken of in an earlier chapter. It may sometimes be necessary to read a whole book in one week in the course of preparing one sermon. A man is to preach, for example, on race relations, and at the last minute some book falls into his hands which it would be foolish for him not to know before he proceeds; or he may have to read pages of church history, or several chapters of philosophy, to present, reinforce, and properly illustrate what he wants to say next Sunday. Whenever such special work is necessary he should do it, not grudgingly, but with the consciousness that no preparation can be too complete if it results in a better sermon. But except for instances of this sort the less a man reads for the sermon just ahead of him and the more he fills his mind with the stuff that will go into any and all sermons, the better a preacher he will become. There is a long preparation and there is a short one. The short one is for next Sunday; the long one is for the next forty years.

It is easy to tell the man who has made the long preparation from the man who has not. In one of Dr. Atkins' sermons I noted references to poetry, painting, music, philosophy, manufacturing, architecture, history; to Greece, Rome, Palestine, Egypt, the Renaissance; to Plato, Frost, Wordsworth, Beethoven, Rembrandt, Handel, Tennyson, St. Gaudens, Watts, Ruskin, Dickens. In one of Dr. Hough's I noted references to Dante, Bunyan, Tennyson, Donald Hankey, Lucretius, Nietzsche, Epicurus, Coulter, Jacks, Homer, and to Barbour's *Life of Alexander Whyte.* In one of Dr. Stamm's, similar references or allusions to Schweitzer, Glover, Carlyle, Browning, Shakespeare, John Wesley's *Journal,* Bunyan's *Pilgrim's Progress,* Byron's "The Prisoner of Chillon," Ibsen's Brand, Tennyson's "Northern Farmer," Barbour's *Life of Alexander Whyte,* Jack's *Religious Perplexities,* Fitch's *None So Blind,* and Homer's *Iliad.*. Yet none of these sermons seemed overloaded. The many references were not lugged in, they all "belonged," because they belonged to the men who wrote the sermons. Even if a preacher makes no quotations and no references or allusions to historical characters or events, you can always tell whether he has made the long preparation. He gives you the impression of having more in him than he has said.

The phrase "popular preacher" is sometimes used in an opprobrious sense. No doubt there is a cheap popularity that is a reproach rather than a compliment. It is also a comfort to some of us to think that our stuff is a little too good to be popular, but we may be mistaken about that. Not all popular things are cheap; not all dull things are good. Let the preacher have his ideal and stick to it. But after that, let him be as popular as he can. To be popular is only to appeal to many people, and that is what every preacher wants to do. Certainly few if any of us need to strive for unpopularity; enough of that will come to us.

Two or three other simple things may help in this matter of preparation. The first is to keep in mind, while one is writing, certain representative persons of one's congregation. I used sometimes to write down the names of several such persons at the head of the sheet on which I began my outline. I had no animus against these persons, I did not preach at them. But they were persons who had recently been in trouble, or whose intellectual or social attitude was a problem to me. They stood for classes or kinds of people — what pleased or helped them would do the same for many others. To have them clearly in mind as representatives of classes of people who needed certain definite things done for them would keep me from getting more interested in my subject than in my people and help me to be concrete and specific.

A similar help is to ask oneself, before one makes his outline for a sermon, " Exactly what do I want to accomplish by this sermon? " It is understood of course that a man knows all the while what he is doing and why he is doing it; and I am not implying that he does not. Yet sometimes a preacher will get hold of a subject that interests him and will play around with it till something comes out on paper or in the pulpit, but he has not handled the thing from start to finish with the one purpose of accomplishing a definite result for his people. The result he aims at may not always be a tremendous, a world-beating one. It may be to enforce some particular duty, or to induce a given mood in his hearers, or to clarify their ideas at a certain point. Whatever the purpose the preacher cannot have it too clearly in mind. If one listens to a sermon and has to ask himself afterwards, "What was he trying to do to me?" something is wrong. If the preacher knows exactly what he wants to do in a sermon, he can ask himself after he gets it written whether he has accomplished his purpose or not; if he has not he can generally go back and do so before it is too late. But nobody can hew to a line which he doesn't see.

It is often well to say over to oneself, out loud, certain parts of his sermon which he wishes to get as nearly perfect as he can. I have known one or two preachers who went to their churches on Saturday nights and preached their sermons through to an imaginary congregation. This procedure would smack too much of unreality for most men; they would hardly be able to preach the sermon through for thinking of what they were doing. But I once heard it said that the best way to teach literature was merely to have it properly read before the class. When one reads poetry he hears in imagination how it sounds; or if he wishes to get the last drop of beauty out of it he reads aloud — indeed, if it is very beautiful he can hardly keep from doing so. We know how a thing we have written will sound by applying the test of "the inner ear." But we know it a good deal better when we have actually heard it. In his own study the preacher can say parts of the sermon to himself without needing to convict himself of egotism, and by such practice he will almost certainly improve himself. It is all very well to say, "I am interested in ideas and in general impressions, and such fooling around with details seems to me mere pottering." It is also proper to remember that one of the greatest artists of the world said, "Perfection is made up of trifles, but perfection is no trifle." I am assuming that every preacher wishes to make every sermon he preaches as good as he can. Why should one put up a good house and paint it a good color, but leave two or three spots on the front unpainted?

Nor will it do for a man to say, "My style is just naturally not good." If so, there is all the more reason to take pains with it. The good writers are not necessarily those who began by being such. When Darwin's *Origin of Species* appeared, one reason it received so good a reading was because the style was as clear and beautiful as the subject matter would permit. Yet Darwin had a terrible time with his style, and once said that if there was any way of saying a thing which was more awkward or obscure than any other way, that was the way it naturally occurred to him to say it. "The style is the man"; but a good style is a man at his best, not at his most careless or slovenly.

Apropos of the matter of brevity or condensation, I once crossed out one hundred and twenty-one words from a sermon that had been handed in by a member of my homiletics class. I felt apologetic about such a drastic procedure, as the man was a good student and a good writer. He came back the next day, commended me for my criticism, and said, "I took out four hundred and thirty-seven more words. I hadn't noticed I used so many words I didn't need."

Like many of us, this same man had a favorite word — "somehow." He could hardly get through a paragraph without it. "Somehow" is not a good word, except in the occasional place where it is needed; it adds indefiniteness to whatever one says. But he used it constantly. Manners have

improved since Shakespeare's time. Rosalind says to Orlando, "Very good orators, when they are out, they will
spit." This man, when he was out, said, "Somehow." He
hadn't noticed this habit. Most of us, as I said, have such
favorite words. If a man says "the very spot," "the very
man," "the very idea," and never says spot or man or idea
without "very," the fact probably is that he doesn't mean
"very" and doesn't know he is saying it. It is just a habit.
The use of such habitual words may be good; they may indicate exactly what the speaker wants to say; but they may
also creep in without his knowing it. It is at least safe to
watch out for them.

In my remarks about vocabulary on an earlier page I did
not mean to imply that vocabulary is of no account; it is of
much account if it is part and parcel of the man, like the
other elements in his style. Whether it is natural or acquired
it helps to reveal the man. If it is native to him it shows
what kind of man he is; if acquired, what kind of man
he thinks it would be nice to be. In the published sermons of one American divine I note the following words:
mystery, hovers, poignant, fleetingness, evanescence, quest,
unveiled, yearning, winsomeness, forefeel, insight, lyric
love, dross-drained, tarries, yonder side, unresting continuity,
unutterable. Any word in this list any preacher might use
occasionally. But these words, if they occur often enough
in the sermons of any man to attract one's attention, indicate that his mind is of a certain turn. He is an imagina-
tive man, poetical, aesthetic, fastidious, and interested in the
creation of what Clive Bell calls "significant form." You
would be surprised to find a man who habitually used these

or similar words, intent in his sermons upon producing a perfectly definite and concrete result. If Dwight Moody did not use such words it was not because he was not familiar with them; it was because they did not suit his purpose. The preacher who uses the short, stubby, unpoetical word, whose vocabulary would be entirely familiar to the harness maker or the clerk in the five-and-ten, is not necessarily a man without literary taste or power. He may be at home with Shakespeare and prefer *The Faerie Queene* to the mystery story; but he chooses to use in his sermons his Anglo-Saxon, matter-of-fact, prosaic vocabulary because he wishes to bring home to ordinary people truth dressed in clothes that make it recognizable at a glance. And whereas the man who uses the more ethereal, aesthetic, deodorized vocabulary gives you the impression of having hunted for his words, like a collector for old china, and of being more interested in the clothes than in the body inside them, the man who uses the short, stubby and familiar words does not seem consciously to have chosen them; rather they appear to have been dictated by his material and his purpose in speaking. You never feel like saying to him — as you often do to the other — what the queen said to Polonius, "More matter with less art."

CHAPTER SIX

A CHAPTER IN BETWEEN

HOWEVER MUCH we might wish it were otherwise, the question of material for sermons is vitally affected by the fact that we have practically no sinners in our congregations. There is a sense of course in which we are all sinners. But of bona fide, genuine, honest-to-God sinners, of men who do wrong because they prefer it or because it is profitable, of men who have not had some experience of salvation, there are very few in our congregations. We preach not wholly to church members but almost entirely to people who are essentially Christian.

This fact, as I said, determines the material for much of our preaching. We do not generally intend to convert. Not but that we would be glad to convert, but we haven't anybody before us who needs converting. What then do they need? They need broadening, refining, educating. They need to be shown the implications of a religion they already profess. They need to be made more tolerant, more progressive, more liberal, more just in their daily conduct, more intelligent about their religion. And always they need to be encouraged. The preacher is not a spiritual " jollier." Pollyannaism is anathema; a cheap optimism turns the stomach. But people need encouragement. If there is anything in religion — any long look into the past and into the future by which the data of the moment may be more fairly judged, any fundamental conviction about the universe, against which all merely temporary movements and tendencies can be seen in a new light, any alleviating consideration to be put down against the grief of the hour, any " balm in Gilead " — people need them all. The preacher will look for such material for his sermons — unless, to be sure, he feels that the way to make people better is to make them feel worse.

But what lies beyond any particular things the preacher can say to put heart into people is his own temperament. It is a great thing for any man, but especially for any man who preaches the gospel, to have a sane, wholesome, cheerful attitude toward life. It is hard for a pessimistic man to cheer folks up much. As Emerson says in his essay, " Self Reliance," " A man cannot deny himself." The fact that people need to be encouraged is what gives extreme humanism so hard a row to hoe. The call to arise and make the best we can out of the worst of all possible worlds without any help from anybody will have to be addressed to a generation less in need of discouragement than we are, before it will meet with any general enthusiastic response.

After a man has preached ten years to any congregation, what is the one thing he will most surely have left in their memory? Individual things he has said will be forgotten; but his temperament, his slant on things, his primary reaction toward God and man, his way of reacting to the joys and sorrows of life — these will remain. People will think of him years later and say, " He would have felt thus and so about this." For years to come they will have been made brave or cowardly, cheerful or depressed, content with the world as it is or determined to make it better, by this bequest of the preacher's temperament. When a man becomes thoroughly discouraged about the world or the church or himself, no matter how eloquent or learned he still is, it is time for him to quit preaching.

The question often arises whether a man should preach an old sermon or write a new one. The present feeling is much against the preaching of an old one. So far as such preaching is a mere escape from the labor of production, the self-respecting preacher will avoid it as he would any other temptation to laziness. But it is not always that. One has a sermon on which, three or four years ago, he worked hours and hours; this week he hasn't any hours at all for working on a sermon. Beecher once said that he could take any sermon he had preached within the last six months and preach it again, changing nothing except the illustrations, and nobody would recognize it. This is an incidental tribute to the value of the illustration. But what if someone should recognize it? The preacher is sometimes in a mood — perhaps from the reading of some book, or the occurrence of some events in his own life or in that of his parish — which makes the writing of one particular sermon inevitable. He may never again be in circumstances that enable him to produce on the same topic another sermon so good as the one he then prepared. If it is a topic to which the attention of people should be directed more than once — and what topic is worth preaching upon that is not worth preaching upon more than once? — why should he preach an inferior sermon because it is new instead of a better one because it is old? We read the same poems and hear the same music over and over. The preacher is neither a poet nor a musician, yet even he should at his best produce things that are worth being heard more than once. Thomas Chalmers and Phillips Brooks used to preach old sermons over again without excuse or comment. One of Phillips Brooks' parishioners once said of one of his sermons, "Oh yes, that is a favorite with us at Trinity." Probably we are too afraid of preaching old sermons. Only, of course, a sermon when it is preached again must also be born again. By rereading, reworking, rewriting, the preacher must make it as new and fresh to himself as it was the first time he preached it.

In general there are no "tricks of the trade" in preaching. Yet there are approaches which, if they do not become habits, have value. Burris Jenkins has a New Year's sermon entitled, "Undaunted by Decembers," in which he repeats six times the quatrain,

> Undaunted by Decembers
> The sap is faithful yet.
> The giving earth remembers,
> And only men forget.

He has no text, but he does with this little verse what preachers have often done with a text. The repetition does not seem monotonous. Repetition in fact is a fine tool — only a man must not use it without intending to, and when he does use it there must be obvious advantage in it. After I had finished this sermon of Dr. Jenkins' and laid the book down, I found myself saying to myself, "Undaunted by Decembers." I did not at once recall the whole four lines, but I was not content till I went back to the book and memorized them. The entire sermon is fine, but what will stay with me is those four lines. However, when I discovered Dr. Jenkins doing the same thing in another sermon it did not seem quite so successful, perhaps because the verse used was a little longer and not quite so easy to remember, perhaps because the freshness and originality of the procedure were a little diminished for me. I found myself saying, "Grand, but not too often. Not a habit."

What place have quotations in a sermon? That depends on what sort of quotations they are and what one uses them for. In a sermon once published in the *Christian Century Pulpit* I counted twenty-four prose quotations, some of them long. Hardly one of them was notable for either form or content. They added no authority to the preacher's message, many of them coming from men of no reputation. There was scarcely a thing in any of them which the preacher himself could not have said as well or better. They gave the impression that the preacher was not preaching but quoting. They had a scrap bag, patchwork effect. Yet there is a kind of quotation — it must be pat, it should not be long nor more difficult to understand than the preacher's own words — that lets light into a passage like a window opening into a dark hallway. For such quotations one does not have to look. They force themselves upon one as the appropriate and perfect thing for the place. I once heard a preacher, speaking on the parable of the Publican and the Pharisee in the Temple, quote three or four lines from Burns' "Holy Willie's Prayer." Someone asked him afterwards, "How did you come to think of that quotation for that place?" He replied,

"I don't know. It just came to me. It's the only one, isn't it?" Quotations belong in some sermons more than in others. And the fact that in those sermons in which we are most in earnest we speak most in our own words and least in the words of someone else, is significant. What the people want to hear, if they want to hear him at all, is the preacher himself and not somebody else.

I am sometimes asked whether the preacher should use the first personal pronoun in his sermons. There is an impersonal use of "I," in which people see at once that the preacher refers to himself not because he wishes to talk about himself but because he knows himself better than he knows anyone else. A preacher is either conceited or he is not. If he is not, people will not consider him so just because he says "I"; and if he is, people will know it anyhow. If he is known to be a modest man he can refer to his own experience as often as he pleases, without offense. Besides, as Professor Cooley somewhere says, people do not object to a man's obtruding his own personality if the personality is acceptable and not obnoxious.

Sermons used commonly to be divided into expository, textual, and topical. I suppose they can still be so divided, though we no longer pay much attention to the division. There are texts which give its natural structure to any sermon — texts like "Ye shall know the truth and the truth shall make you free"; or, "Man shall not live by bread alone but by every word that proceedeth out of the mouth of the Lord." How can one preach from this latter text, for instance, without discussing first the bread and inquiring how it happens that so many people in the world about us do not have even bread; and second, asking what is meant by " words that proceed out of the mouth of the Lord," whether there are any such words these days, and how it is that one lives by them? In other words the text itself suggests the structure of the sermon — first the material things, then the spiritual, and finally the relation between these two in human life.

When a text thus suggests the structure of the sermon the preacher will naturally take the hint. But the old idea that there is some sacredness or authority about a sermon developed in this fashion out of a text has disappeared, along with the older conception of the Bible. Likewise — only even more completely — has the idea vanished that if one can take a passage, say of one of Paul's epistles, clear away misunderstandings, explain obscurities, and arrive at the apostle's exact meaning, he will have come into possession of a divine and authoritative word not otherwise to be found. Outside of fundamentalist circles people are not much interested in such expositions; they do not particularly care what St. Paul meant.

Neither the expository nor the textual sermon has any advantage over any other kind. It is not always necessary to have a text. Our uniform use of it is more or less an unconscious concession to tradition. If a text helps one, as it often does, let him use it; if it does not help him, but he wants to prefix it to his sermon as a sort of motto, let him do that. But if he doesn't want to make use of any text, why should he? Unless the text is of help there is no loss in its absence — except, of course, that the congregation may feel that something is lacking. Whether it is worth while to concede to this feeling and hunt the concordance through for a text after the sermon is written is a question each minister will answer for himself. To preach without a text whenever that seems to be the natural thing to do may indirectly help people to a more discriminating attitude toward the Bible.

Most sermons these days are " topical "; that is, the preacher has in mind something that he wants to preach about. It is the subject itself that appeals to him, not its setting in any biblical passage. The subject may not have come to him from the reading of either the Bible or any other book, but from the newspaper or a magazine article; it may have been suggested by some conversation, or by his having had to wait an hour on the street corner for his wife who said she would be there and wasn't, or by a strike or a lockout in his city, or by any one of a hundred other circumstances. Except for the consideration I have elsewhere urged — namely, the kind and amount of education that lies in up-to-date biblical preaching — there is no reason I can see why a man should waste his time trying to tie up what he says to some biblical text, especially when the more discerning among his hearers easily see that his text is an afterthought. There is no need to apologize for or to call attention to the absence of a text. Most people will not notice its absence. Let a man proceed to say what he has to say, as anyone outside the pulpit would do.

Except in the Episcopal Church, the Protestant church is not supposed to have a " church year." Yet from the beginning the pulpit has generally taken account of Christmas and Easter. In recent years certain other days have become almost as insistent in their demand for recognition: Memorial day; Armistice day; Ash Wednesday, if the preacher is sufficiently impressed with the value of observing Lent; Mothers' day, if he is sufficiently sentimental or willing to capitalize on the propaganda of the newspapers, the Western Union, and the florists; Washington's birthday, or Lincoln's, if either of these falls on Sunday and if the preacher can make use of them; Labor day, generally. The increasing number of these special days is already an embarrassment to the preacher who has enough to say without them. One hopes the increase will not go on indefinitely. There has been some attempt to add Fathers' day to Mothers' day. Badly as father may need a day dedicated to him, I hope he will have to do without it, else we shall presently have also a Willie's day and a Grandmothers' day and a Sarah's day, and so on through the family.

What shall one do with the special days already instituted? Use them so far as he can profitably do so, and forget them when he prefers. Some he can hardly ignore, or will naturally even wish to use, if they fall on Sunday. Now that so few churches have their own services on Thanksgiving day and so few people attend the union services on that day, the preacher may well preach a Thanksgiving sermon on the Sunday before Thanksgiving day. It seems natural to preach a Memorial day sermon when that day falls on Sunday; otherwise perhaps generally not. While the question of war and peace is so vividly before the world, one welcomes Armistice day as an opportunity to speak his mind on this vital matter. The year's events will on each Armistice day give him something to say which he did not and could not say the year before.

Of some of the other days which come around every year the same cannot be said. It is not so easy to have something new to say on each Christmas or on each Easter Sunday. Fortunately, on these days the sermon is less in the foreground than on most Sundays of the year. Easter is the choir's day. Its spirit is conveyed to worshipers better by music — the right sort of music — than by any message the preacher can bring. Let him not on that account shirk what he has to say about life, death, and immortality; on the contrary, let him welcome the chance to say things he could hardly say at any other time. But there is no Sunday in the year when less of a sermon is needed than on Easter. Let the choir sing itself out and let the preacher then take what time is left and be grateful for it.

The same in less degree applies to Christmas. There is a spirit to Christmas that doesn't go with any other day in the year. The main thing for the preacher to do is to get himself into that spirit in time to create a sermon out of it. If he is still a young man and his children are growing up around him and his own imagination is still alive, the task is easy. It helps, also, to read some of the great Christmas stories, like Dickens' *Christmas Carol*. I have often found that the best preparation for a Christmas sermon is wandering around the streets, especially in a big city, the week before Christmas. I have made more than one Christmas sermon out of the toys, gadgets, dummy orchestras, electric trains, and similar objects of art and interest that crowd the store windows.

I have got one by just standing for two hours, on Wednesday or Thursday before Christmas Sunday, on the busiest corner in the downtown district, watching people come and go, listening to what parents said to their children and children to their parents, letting my imagination run freely, and taking a good bath in the stream of human nature that flowed by. I got a still better one by conducting two boys, aged five and seven years, through the big downtown stores, letting them look till they couldn't look any longer, riding up and down the escalators with them, hearing them tell what they would buy if they had all the money they wanted, or what they would do with it if they had all the candy in the world, going with them into the Zeppelin, watching their reaction toward other children of their own age who had more money, or less, to spend than they did.

I have gone from one auction room to another at Christmas time, taking note of the kind of people who were there and what they were after. I have listened to men casting horoscopes, and to men in the parking lots selling stabilizers that would make a car run as well on two cylinders as on six and auto polish guaranteed to keep a shine on your car till next Christmas. In short I have given myself as much of a pre-Christmas spree as a sober man with a reputation to maintain can allow himself; and as a mine of material for Christmas sermons I have found this quite equal to anything in the Gospels. To be sure, I have tried not to divorce it from the spirit of the Gospels; but Christmas is a human day. It is bigger than a merely Christian day; it has a lot of good wholesome heathenism about it. The best way to get a sermon for it is not to sit in one's study and brood about it, but to plunge into the human stream as it flows by the door.

A Christmas or Easter sermon does not need to be profound, for on such days people are not in a profound mood. It needs to belong, to embody the spirit of the season. If it can sanctify that spirit a little, show what Christian and spiritual implications are wrapped up in it, and add the one touch which can come from the pulpit and from nowhere else — that is all that is needed. But an Easter or Christmas sermon that might have been preached on any other Sunday is no good. I have tried to indicate some ways in which the stuff that goes into a Christmas sermon can be varied from year to year. In spite of that no man can preach an equally good, new Christmas sermon, every year, nor is there any reason why he should try to do so. If he writes three good Christmas sermons in ten years I should say he has done pretty well. With three good sermons on hand he can preach them by turns and give people three years in which to forget the sermon they have just heard — an interval much longer than most folks need for forgetting.

Series of sermons present both an opportunity and a problem. Their advantage is their continuity. If they are successful the congregation should be larger and more attentive toward the end of the series than at the beginning. Incidentally, such a scheme saves the minister much time in preparation and for five or six weeks prevents his worrying about the choice of a subject. The trouble with sermons in series is that one cannot always tell what people will be interested in. To advertise six sermons on a certain theme and find at the end of the third that people do not care for it is to find oneself in a box. I have once or twice abandoned a series of sermons in the middle. While I have not been proud of this performance, it has never wholly destroyed my reputation with my people. Perhaps they credited me with more independence and courage, certainly with more humanity, than if I had dragged them on to the bitter end.

At certain seasons of the year, especially during Lent, sermons in series can be made more profitable than sermons whose topics are selected at random. Scenes from the life of Jesus, the parables, the great doctrines of the church, with a sermon on immortality for Easter, provide a never failing resource and make a cumulative impression. At the other seasons of the year, especially for the Sunday evening service, series of sermons on social questions, or on individual or family life, or on some of the great intellectual or artistic or scientific movements of the time, or on great characters either of the present or of the past, or on the eight or ten best sellers of the season — all give the preacher a chance to produce a continuous and growing impression upon his hearers.

I seem to have assumed here that there will be an evening service. To be sure, in many churches nowadays there is none; but I think that in general there ought to be. Many preachers spend Sunday evening with their young people. To do that is well and good, provided it is not merely an excuse for not doing something which will cost more labor. No ordinary preacher can produce two equally good sermons every Sunday the year round. The trouble with most Sunday evening services is that they are a mere repetition of the morning service, except that they are a little poorer in all respects: the congregation is made up of the same people, only fewer of them; the choir sings the same sort of music, only with less interest and effectiveness; the preacher talks about the same sort of thing, only with less preparation, more boredom and greater evidence of fatigue.

Not much is to be said for an evening service of this kind. But there are hundreds of people in every community who have not been to church in the morning. There are endless topics that need to be discussed, matters vital to the life of the individual and the community, but not quite of the kind one wants to preach about in the morning. There is a way of speaking, a little more informal, a little less careful as to mere literary form, which suits such subjects and the people who will come to hear them commented on. These things furnish the preacher with his opportunity for evening services. It is true that such services pretty nearly double the amount of time and labor that go into production each week, but at the same time they exercise the ingenuity of the preacher; they give him practice in speaking to people who are not gospel-soaked and they greatly enlarge the scope of his own interests and of his popular appeal. A man should be very sure, before he gives up his evening service, that he is not doing so merely because it is much the easiest way. Even among the saints laziness is still the original sin. President Kirkland of Harvard said of John Adams, "For fifty years he rose before the sun." Modern life hardly encourages this habit, at least in town. But there is no law against a man's sitting up as long as he wants to after the sun goes down. I am assuming that the conscientious preacher, year in and year out, will put into his work about all the energy he has.

If a preacher has never tried his hand at the "book sermon" I would advise him to do so. Rightly done it is not a mere book review — though the hearers will get an idea of the content of the book and of the preacher's reaction to it — but a sermon based upon and growing out of the book. One will usually give in his own words the story told in the book. For a preacher to whom extemporaneous speaking is difficult, this is the finest kind of practice. The thread of the story keeps him on the track. He has no nervousness about losing his way. His choice of words and the formation of his sentences are as free as they can be in any kind of public speaking. This practice may easily develop in him a more extemporaneous manner which will be of advantage in his more formal sermons.

For the book sermon one will generally choose novels, because they are what people read. This choice will often give opportunity to commend a novelist who is not so popular as he deserves to be, or to show up at his true value one whom everybody is reading but who is much overrated. People read uncritically. To help them toward good books and more discriminating reading is amply worth while. To how large a number of people such book sermons can be made to appeal will depend upon many circumstances besides the skill of the preacher, but they are worth doing. If one has no evening service and his conscience hurts him because of it, let him try a series of book sermons.

The day of funeral sermons is happily almost gone by. So far as it meets the approval of his people the preacher will prefer to confine himself, at funerals, to prayer and the reading of appropriate passages of Scripture. Yet many people will not be satisfied with these; they will want the minister to say something of his own. What shall he say? If the person whose funeral he is to conduct has been well known to him there is no great difficulty. In cases of the opposite sort I have often found an easy way out. A good woman comes to ask me to conduct a funeral service for her mother. I say, "Your mother was born in Vermont?" "Oh no," she says, "my mother was born in Scotland. Her people were Covenanters; her father," etc. She is thus started upon a story of her mother's career and a delineation of her character which relieve her own heart and even warm mine. With a hint now and then to draw her back from a detour, or a question to bring out some characteristic so far unmentioned, she talks on for half an hour or more. The next day I merely turn into my own words what she has said to me. The things that people thus tell the minister about their loved ones are exactly the things which the minister, with due selection, omission and emphasis, will want to say at the funeral service.

I have spoken of the preaching of old sermons. Something akin to this though not quite the same is the reworking of old material into new forms for new occasions. I have heard it said, I do not know how truly, that Dr. George A. Gordon was seldom content with speaking once on any topic. He would discuss it first at a midweek meeting, speaking informally and briefly. A few months later it would appear, in better form, as a Sunday evening talk. Within a year or two it would come out on a Sunday morning, this time dressed with all the art and skill that the preacher could muster, and showing clearly the difference between a talk hastily made up and a sermon carefully worked out.

The contemporary pulpit has been much criticized because it says so little about sin. To this criticism two things are to be said. In the first place the pulpit today probably deals as often and as drastically with particular sins, especially the "white collar sins," as it ever did in the past. In earlier times the preacher spent much effort to induce in his people the sense of sin in general — sinfulness at large, so to speak. He was supposed, as part of his spiritual equipment, to have a very keen sense of sin himself. Jonathan Edwards, for example, had it; though had you pinned him down to naming exactly what sins he had committed, the good man would doubtless have been hard put to it to answer. Whittier expresses the same feeling about himself:

> All that the schoolmen say, alas,
> Within myself I know;
> Too black ye cannot paint the sin,
> Too small the merit show —

though few whiter, cleaner souls than that of the Quaker poet could probably be found in any generation. How much good was accomplished by this emphasis upon sin, this creation of the feeling of unworthiness, this attitude that made a man feel worse about himself the better he got, is not easy to say. It probably militated against the danger of spiritual pride; it undoubtedly fitted into the spiritual need of the times, else it would not have appeared. But it certainly does not seem natural these days. In fact it is hard to make it seem otherwise than artificial and manufactured.

Second, it may be said, to those who feel that this lack of emphasis upon sin is a loss in our Christian consciousness and that the preacher should bestir himself to bring it back, that not all aspects of religious truth are or can be equally present and prominent at any one time. If we have lost a sense of sin which we ought to get back then in time we shall get it back. If our present emphasis upon the more positive and objective features of religion is a onesided emphasis, it is no more onesided than the older one on the negative and purely personal features. The conscientious preacher will preach more about sin when he feels he ought to do so. Why should he do so before that? I may add my own conviction that the sense of sin has often been over-cultivated, and not with good results. The people who do not need it take it to heart, while the people who need it and might profit by it throw it away; so that those who already feel worse than they need to, feel still worse, while those who ought to feel bad about themselves continue to feel good.

One ought if possible to avoid sameness in his preaching. Nor is there any great difficulty about this. Variety comes through the preacher's having variety in his own interests. The man whose only interest is the social question will certainly become monotonous; so will any preacher who has but one interest. The man who is constantly enlarging his acquaintance with the history, literature, and philosophy of the Christian religion will have variety enough both in his fundamental themes and in the material by which he illustrates and enforces them. Still, it is well to look back now and then and see just what one has been preaching about for the last three or six months. Listeners may detect sameness, or vaguely feel it, even though the preacher is unconscious of it. All winter, perhaps, the preacher reads books of one kind, say on social questions. Without his knowing it,

> Almost his nature is subdued to what it works in,
> Like the dyer's hand.

It is not enough to be content with such variety as naturally comes; a conscious attempt to avoid monotony, both in matter and style, is always in place.

The titles of sermons are important. One should not be afraid of a commonplace title that states the subject without any attempt to dress it up. If one is to preach about salvation, why not entitle the sermon just " Salvation," or perhaps, " What is Salvation? " — at any rate something perfectly simple which tells what one is to speak about. Titles that sound as if the preacher had hunted for them give the impression that he is more interested in phrases than in the truth they are intended to intimate. On the other hand some men have a genius for good titles that stick in the mind and rouse curiosity. Such a title is Dr. Sockman's, " The Unemployed Carpenter," for a sermon about Jesus preached in a time of unemployment. Dr. Jenkins' titles — " Knee Deep in June," " Youth Haywire? " " Let's Build a New World," " Up a Tree," " Night Flight " — arrest the attention and give a hint not merely of the subject which is to be preached about but of the mood in which it will be treated. One may say — I hope without offense — that Dr. Hough's title, " The Advance to Dialectic," is hardly so good; too many people do not know what dialectic means. Of Dr. Atkins' titles, " Throne Rooms " and " Circles and Orbits," it may perhaps be said that most people have never been in a throne room and have no definite idea of what it is, and that " orbit," however familiar to the student, is a word which carries no definite meaning to the ordinary parishioner. After I had read this sermon I knew exactly what the title meant. But shouldn't a title show what one is going to do before he does it? William James' phrase, "chronic and acute religion," would make a good title; it is picturesque and everybody can see what it means. If one is going to preach on skepticism, agnosticism, and religious faith, he might name his sermon in many ways. Calling it, "How Do We Know?" would cover the ground in words of one syllable.

Some sermons name themselves. If one preaches on the fall of man he calls his sermon "The Fall of Man" and does not look around for anything more spectacular. If he preaches on modernism he can hardly do better than to call his sermon just that. But if he preaches on the different interpretations given to life and religion by different systems and men, and no merely descriptive title occurs to him, he might call the sermon, "Each in His Own Tongue." The title of a well known book or magazine article, like "The Supremacy of the Spiritual," or "The Forgotten Man," or "A Tale of Two Cities," often makes a good sermon title. "Everybody's Christ," one of Dr. Coffin's titles, and "Giants and Grasshoppers," one of Bishop McConnell's, strike one as good titles — they not only name but suggest. When one man announces as his title, "Seven Easter Certainties," and another, "The Great Hunger," you sense a difference between the two men, even before you know that one of them is a great champion of fundamentalism and the other a Jewish rabbi who is really a poet. "Who's To Blame?" is probably a better title than "Responsibility." "How One Man Discovered God" seems to suggest one kind of preacher; "Anchors of the Driven Soul" another kind. A man betrays himself in his titles. However, I would not overemphasize this matter; there are more important things. But if you should write a sermon to which you couldn't give a title you would know that something was wrong. Good titles count.

I was once in a group of ministers, one of whom had been traveling for several months. He had been to church every Sunday. He complained that while most of the sermons he had heard had been interesting, clear, instructive, and so on, only a few of them had "really gripped" him. He seemed to think the proportion was bad. I thought it pretty good. That is, every sermon ought to be clear; no matter how deep or pious or elevating what you say is, if people do not know what it is you have wasted your time. It is like selling a town lot that cannot be located; it's a fraud. Again, most sermons should be to some degree informative. The preacher is a student of religion; he should know more about it than those who listen to him; people should not hear him Sunday after Sunday without having their ideas enlarged, their points of view changed, their minds improved. The preacher is an educator. Most grown people need education in religion as much as children do. A man may have been through the public educational mill from kindergarten to university and have learned practically nothing about religion in the whole process — a fact which, if we were far enough away from it to see it properly, would look both absurd and disgraceful. Therefore educative preaching renders a service even to the educated in American society as now organized. There are few better tests of a preacher's work, especially over a period of years, than the test of its educative quality.

And every sermon should be interesting. Interestingness is the minimum homiletic virtue. People will not listen unless they want to; except for a very short time, they will not even make an effort to listen. And they should not have to do so. The sermon should interest them just as any other interesting thing does, on its own account and without effort on their part. Clear, educative, interesting — all sermons should be these.

But should they all be "gripping"? Not at all. Sometimes, for a sermon to be gripping would defeat its purpose and contradict its mood. Burris Jenkins has a sermon on dogs. He begins with Luke's statement that the dogs came and licked the sores of Lazarus; they were the only friends the poor man had. He tells various dog stories, speaks of the companionship and the understanding of dogs, their courage and endurance, their loyalty, so often greater than the loyalty of men. He almost, or quite, redeems at least one verse of Kipling's preachy "If" by making the last line read,

> And — what is more — you'll be a *dog,* my son.

From the first word to the last the sermon is perfectly clear; it is even informative (which is something to accomplish with such a subject); it is interesting. Not once does your attention threaten to waver. But the sermon does not "grip" you, and it would be a failure if it did. The sermon is intended to throw the listener into a contemplative and appreciative mood, to broaden his interest in the humbler creatures of the earth, to celebrate affection, sympathy, loyalty, to hint at God's interest in subhuman personalities and their possible value for him. To attempt to do these things for the listeners by gripping them, making them sit on the edges of their pews, would defeat its own purpose. It would be like putting a man into the dentist's chair to make him relax.

But there are truths which ought to grip people. When Jonathan Edwards preached his sermon, " Sinners in the Hands of an Angry God," if he hadn't gripped anybody, if people had just sat back and expanded and grown warm and sunshiny as they listened, it would have been a failure. But if people have a strained and overanxious look during your Christmas sermon you may know that that has been a failure. Sermons are preached for many purposes. They are the expression of many different moods in the preacher, and are intended to produce many different moods in the hearers. For a man who likes to think of himself as having a dramatic and Napoleonic control over people it is doubtless a satisfaction — this feeling that he has them in his grip and can squeeze them as hard as he will. But it is not the preacher's only nor highest satisfaction, and it can easily be overdone.

Which leads me to speak of moods in the preacher. We are all creatures of moods. Every man, preacher or otherwise, has also some dominant mood, some mood that comes to him oftener than others and is, as we say, the ruling mood of his life. I have already indicated that the greatest thing a preacher contributes to his people is this dominant mood. It is his great bequest; it is that portion of him which remains with his people after they have forgotten every particular thing he has said to them.

But a man who is not wholly onesided will have many moods, and most of them have a place in sermons. A thing is not necessarily trivial because it is not heavy, nor flippant because it is not serious. I have often felt that no man who is always and only serious ought to go into the ministry. There is enough in the ministry to make him serious even if he is not overly so to begin with. I shall carry with me to my dying day the memory of one good man in my college class who was headed for the ministry and who said in one of our class prayer meetings, " I never do anything without asking myself whether I can do it to the glory of God." He went so far as to particularize; he said he never ate his dessert at dinner without asking himself that question. I submit that a man who goes through life pointing at every piece of pie that comes onto the table and saying to himself, " To the glory of God: yes? no? " is sunk before he starts. I have lost track of this particular good man. Maybe he found a congregation of lighthearted and frivolous people who needed to be wet down once a week, and so fulfilled a noble function. Maybe later on he himself smiled. Maybe God sent him a wife with a sense of humor and gave him children who played around in the sunshine and climbed over him and laughed.

However that may be, one great source of monotony and even of dreariness in sermons is the idea that they should all be dug out of the same mood. A mere joker has no place in the pulpit — for that matter he hasn't much place anywhere. And there are few such men. Most great humorists have had, besides their humor, a great power of indignation and a great gift for the serious statement of serious things. But in the pulpit as outside it " God fulfills himself in many ways." One of the best tests of a sermon is, Does it produce in the hearers the same mood out of which it grew in the preacher's mind? But people need many moods to live by. They often do need to be made more serious; they even need, sometimes, to be made to feel bad. But they also need to be loosened up, lightened, cheered, and sent on their way rejoicing.

There are moods that should not be embodied in any sermon. It is agreed, for instance, that the minister should never scold. The people who are present seldom need scolding. But here the matter of temperament comes in again. Probably no preacher intends to scold; but if he is the scolding kind he may do so without knowing it. I recently heard a sermon about complaining. The preacher said we should not complain, and his sermon was a forty-minute complaint of those who complain.

The discouraged mood, likewise, is always out of place — though the preacher will often be discouraged. When he is, let him get out a sermon he wrote when he wasn't discouraged. The world is damp enough already. Nor does the cynical mood belong in the pulpit, though the preacher may now and then have a touch of cynicism. He may occasionally sprinkle upon his sermon a drop of such cynicism as unavoidably distills itself in his soul — just as one drops a little cayenne pepper upon his roast beef. But a sermon made out of cynicism is like a house whose foundations have been eaten by the termites.

The angry mood will not naturally lend itself to sermons — though the preacher who is never angry, and who does not know what things in this old world he should be angry about, is lacking somewhere. But except for those moods which we recognize as improper, or as proper to be entertained for the moment only, there is no mood that comes to the preacher which he cannot use in his sermons. The more vivid, the more intense, and the more variegated his moods, the better will his preaching be.

In sermons as in other literary or artistic creations there is a quality which we call " reality." It is not the mere absence of pretense or make-believe. It is something that gives one's hearers the feeling that he is dealing not with ideas or propositions and thoughts, but with things themselves. Any habit of speech that interferes with this sense of reality is of the evil one. I have occasionally heard a preacher close his sermon with the remark, " I leave these few thoughts with you "; I always feel like saying to him, " Oh, take them along." I warn against such usages because I feel that most preachers do have the sense of reality in what they are saying, and that it is generally only some bad mannerism of speech that gives the opposite impression. One gets it now and then from the fact that a sermon is overdressed, or overpainted, or too pretty. Whenever you feel that the preacher is primarily intent not upon what he is saying but upon how he is saying it, and that he is relying for his impression not upon the truth which he utters but upon the words in which he clothes it, you get this sense of unreality. When you go out of the church and onto the pavement, where the actual sun shines on you and actual people bump into you, you come down to earth again. During the sermon you were somewhere else.

If one asks how this sense of unreality is to be avoided and the sense of reality to be gained, the answer is easy: Let a man preach about what he is sure of and what is important.

Young preachers are often so impressed with the things they no longer believe, and yet so anxious to avoid the expression of doubt, that there doesn't seem to be much left for them to preach about. But there must be some true things that are also important. Let a man get hold of some such thing and begin with it. There is, surely, a line between right and wrong. This line is certainly important — about the most important thing there is. After a man has discarded all his beliefs about heaven and hell, it is still true, and still tremendously important, that the issues of life are glorious if the life is good, dreadful beyond utterance if it is bad. Dr. Gordon has somewhere a phrase, "The deep tragedy of man's life upon the earth." Life is a tragic thing, not in the sense that it must end sadly, but in the sense that its issues either way are tremendous. Wickedness is a reality, goodness is equally a reality. Injustice is as a fire that burns in the vitals of society. Consequences are sure. Let a man soak himself in these realities of life. When he gets up to speak let him not "submit a few thoughts" to his hearers, but set the naked reality before them just as he sees and feels it himself, and he will have reality in his preaching. But a man who preaches about things he only half feels and that do not greatly matter to himself will lose such reality as he started with.

There are many things that are tremendously important when you stop to think of them, but which people do not always stop to think about. It is part of the preacher's business to show their importance. Horace Bushnell has a famous sermon on "Unconscious Influence." Read the title and you are likely to say to yourself, "It can't be very important if we are unconscious of it." Read the sermon and you see that it is exactly the fact that we are unconscious of it that makes it important. You feel also that the preacher has not been submitting a few thoughts for your inspection; he has brought you face to face with a great reality. For the time being, at least, nothing in the world looks truly important except one's unconscious influence. I don't know any way to attain this quality of reality in preaching, except for a man to preach always about something which at least for the time is greatly important to him, to understand clearly that words are only an introduction to things, and to use them as such. Perhaps this is sufficient.

Some preachers are worried about originality in their sermons, and they therefore strive to be original. But that is the way to become queer, bizarre, unpredictable, but not original. In the last analysis the only originality there is for a man is just to be himself. If God made him like most other men, then he has to be that way. But he never is absolutely like anyone else, and the difference, however slight, may be extremely significant. To try to be like anybody else is not to try to be original but to try to be a copy. Every effort for originality is a renunciation of it. If a man will accept himself for what he is, and will polish himself off so that the spots in which he is different will show, he will have originality enough. Most unpolished stones look about alike; the difference comes out in the polishing.

A preacher may well ask himself as he finishes a sermon or a paragraph, "Is that or isn't it just the way everybody would say it?" If it is, the escape is not in trying to say the thing in a way naturally foreign to him. Let him dig down into his own mind and see if, when he gets clear down to himself, there is not something there that impels him to speak in a way peculiar to himself. If a man will forget the matter of originality and just deal a little more deeply with himself, he will have what originality God meant him to have. Besides, originality is not always all to the good; it may be obnoxious as well as attractive. But all consciously acquired originality is sure to be obnoxious.

There is an old distinction concerning which another word may perhaps be said by way of making it more clear. It is that between the essay and the pulpit style of speaking. The essay is a third-person affair, written by one man to be read by whoever will read it. But the writer does not know who will read it; he does not address himself to anyone in particular. It is not a face-to-face affair. It is entirely possible to write in this manner a sermon in which the ideas are sound and the style clear, and in which even conviction and passion are present. What keeps it from being a sermon is only the fact that it is an essay.

One may take as an illustration the closing paragraph (the rest of the sermon is in the same style) of a sermon published in one of Joseph Fort Newton's volumes of *Best Sermons*. The paragraph is a description of Baron von Hügel. "He was a student of religion. . . . There was no provincialism in his outlook. . . . He presented the spiritual treasures of the ancient church. . . . It is safe to predict that when the day arrives. . . . Meanwhile our task is to learn. . . ." This is from anybody to anybody. There is one "we" in it, as if the speaker suddenly felt that there was someone there besides himself; but this might be the social "we" as well as the personal one, meaning society at large. There is no appeal, no direct address. If the sermon had not been printed in a book of sermons none would suspect it of being one. It might quite as well be an article quoted from the *Forum*. When one turns on the other hand to the closing passages in Rabbi Emil G. Hirsch's sermon, "Alone with Thee, My God," he finds a different atmosphere: "Oh, Sinai congregation, your name will be inscribed. . . . Let your conscience speak. . . . Take heed, the day of reckoning is coming. Your callousness, your social splendor, your mimicry and imitation of what others do will not protect you. You think that you can escape. No one escapes. Change your name, the record is established and known. Change your religion and associations. . . . Sinai congregation, high priest of Judaism today, of liberal Judaism, alone into the sanctuary of thy God. Ask pardon for thyself, thy brothers, thy people. . . . Alone with Thee, my God. Alone with thee, Israel stand firm and fast. Sinai congregation, to thy tents." The feeling here is deep and true, but not necessarily any more so than in the other sermon. What is here that is not in the other, however, is the face-to-face speech of one man to other men. It is almost as if he called them by name or held them by the hand. It is, so far as form goes, the difference between the essay and the sermon.

It might be said that if a man is deeply in earnest about the truth he is speaking he will speak in this latter way. But that is not necessarily true because of the obvious fact that some very earnest men do speak in the essay manner.

I believe — unless of course a man is persuaded that the essay style is better — that it is necessary to be on one's guard to make sure that one speaks in the direct way natural to the sermon. A man who has any habit of self-criticism can catch himself when he wanders into the easier, more indirect, less personal style, and can bring himself back. By all means let him do so. "There is joy in heaven over one sinner that repenteth."

This matter of the essay versus the sermon style is not the only point at which a man should watch himself, or at which he can influence his own manner of writing and speaking even if he has been long at it. If one fears that his vocabulary is too scholastic let him try the experiment of writing a sermon in words of one syllable. He will not be quite able to do it — at least I have never been able to, though I have tried it more than once. Let him make an exception of prepositions like "under," "over," "besides," two-syllable words for which there are no substitutes. Let him say just what he wants to, not sidle off for the sake of using a short word instead of a long one. Except for these, let him say it all in words of one syllable. Let him say "but" instead of "nevertheless" or "however"; "great" instead of "stupendous"; "I know it" instead of "I am cognizant of it"; "dig it out by the roots" instead of "eradicate it," and so on. He will not wholly succeed, as I said, but he will be surprised at how near he can come to success. And in the process he may become convinced that the short word is better than the long one. If he is not convinced, then of course for him it is not better; but if he is, he will have made a start toward a good habit.

This experiment may do one other thing for him. It may show him that profound truth can be put in simple language and that the average congregation is quite capable of taking it in when it is so put. Some ministers underestimate the intellectual capacity of their congregations, when the fault lies really with themselves. I was once surprised to read in one of President Eliot's essays that the Pilgrim Mothers did not know how to read. Dr. Eliot went on to say that this did not indicate on their part a smaller degree of intelligence than the Pilgrim Fathers had; it merely indicated that in their time, reading and writing were not part of feminine education. He said that the women were quite able to discuss the content of the sermon with the men at the Sunday dinner table, though they could not have read it had it been put before them in print.

In the same way, a congregation may be made up largely of unschooled persons. School-words, terms not in common use, involved sentences such as are not usual in ordinary conversation, philosophical language, may stand in their way. But words are one thing and ideas are another. Any idea that is important for any Christian congregation it can get without difficulty or strain if the idea is put simply enough. If I may be pardoned for so personal an illustration (I am a modest man, see p. 122), I was once pastor of a university congregation for ten years, and for six years after that preached to a congregation that had been gathered through a quarter of a century by a man who always preached the most solid kind of stuff and never made any concession to the intellectual weaknesses of his hearers. There were some ordinary people in this group, to be sure, but the head and front of it were schoolteachers, university professors, editors, doctors, lawyers, literary people, and others of the intelligentsia. From this latter place I went to preach to a big miscellaneous congregation of undistinguished people, only a small proportion of whom were college or university bred. I did not find it necessary to change the subjects of my sermons or the substance of my preaching, at least consciously. I found that this congregation was entirely able to absorb what are sometimes regarded as abstract or difficult ideas, such as the reasons for a theistic interpretation of the universe, the criticism of naturalistic philosophies, the general idea of relativity, the monistic as against the pluralistic philosophy, the idea of the objectivity of value, and so on. Few ideas — perhaps none at all — that are essential to Christianity, when you get them stripped of the wrong kind of verbiage, are abstract. It is worth while to cultivate a style and vocabulary that permit a man to bring to his congregation the best he has or can get, instead of limiting himself, because of their supposed incapacity, to exhorting them to be good.

Which leads me to say that, not necessarily in every sermon but as often as it can fruitfully be done, the preacher's underlying philosophy ought to be made to stand out. His sermon ought to run up into it or down into it. The minister's beliefs and convictions are thus made to appear, as they are and should be, not isolated remarks about detached things but parts of one whole view of all things. Thus his words are given a grounding and a consequent firmness which they could hardly have otherwise. In my homiletics classes I have sometimes at the close of his sermon asked a student, "Are you a pragmatist, a realist, an intuitionalist, an idealist, a personalist, or what?" If he wonders why I have asked the question I can always tell him honestly that there was nothing in his sermon to indicate what he was. He might be anything or nothing so far as the sermon showed. Yet a man's theology always runs back into his philosophy, and his particular view of any spiritual truth into his general conviction about the universe itself. To give people this general view, this philosophy — not in one sermon devoted to it; they would not get that; it would seem dull and remote to them; but by making his sermon wherever he can issue in it or out of it — may be a more important service to them than at first appears. It may, without their knowing it or calling it by any such big name, get them into the habit of thinking philosophically — by which, of course, I do not mean being interested in epistemology or other technical philosophic questions, but taking a comprehensive and synoptic view of things. Remote as philosophy may seem from practical religion, it has a profound influence upon the spiritual life of thoughtful people.

There is another thing that is akin to this of philosophy but not quite the same. Henry Drummond overworked his idea of "natural law in the spiritual world," and yet it was a suggestive idea, and still is. When one can show that some principle that applies to the personal life applies also to society at large, and back of that even to nature, he has given it a cosmic standing that greatly recommends it. Take for instance such a subject as "The Healing Power." There is a healing power in our personal lives — in our intellectual life something that tells us when we are wrong and how to get right; in our moral life something that shows that we are sick and how to get well. This purely personal or spiritual aspect may be the one on which the preacher wishes to lay stress. But if he will set it off against the same sort of healing power that works in trees and flowers and in the small and insignificant creatures of the earth, enabling the earthworm to grow a new tail or the snail to put out a new horn with a new eye at its tip; that works also in human society, correcting abuses and abolishing excesses; and if he will spend enough time upon this principle to make it an actual demonstration of the presence of the healing power in all nature and in all life, he will have given it a universal standing and made it appear as what it is: a part of the structure of the universe. If in addition, and in accordance with what I said in the paragraph above, he will show that this healing power as it works in nature and in human life is at least one of the things we mean by the word God, he will have made a big subject out of what otherwise, applied merely to the spiritual life of the individual, would have been a small one. I am always exhorting my students to preach on big themes, so that they can be sure of having at least one big thing about their sermons. But anything worth preaching about can be made big if it can be shown to operate or apply not in the personal life alone but in the world at large and to issue in or rest upon a view of the whole.

I have had much to say about production, the ways of it and the amount of it that is demanded of the preacher. Perhaps more important than any of these items is the level of production which a preacher does or does not maintain.

There are many preachers to whom you can listen without being tremendously impressed by any individual sermon, but their general level is high; their work is sustained. Year after year they never fall below a certain high level. They are like those scientists who make no one startling contribution to knowledge but who work patiently, persistently, and successfully to increase the general intelligence; or like engineers who discover no new continents but who build bridges, solid, permanent and beautiful, across the chasms that divide people; or like architects who introduce no new styles, but who put up houses that are at once lovely and serviceable and who never once in their lives build an ugly or insecure or unusable structure. Preachers who maintain a high standard and never fall below it are like these other men, I say; and of them all it may be said, in the words of Ecclesiasticus, "These maintain the fabric of the world, and in the handiwork of their craft is their prayer."

There are also preachers who do astonishingly well upon occasion, but one cannot be sure of them; they do fall down. I suppose one must be the kind of man he is and do the kind of work he can; yet so far as the matter is open to choice, the preachers who never fall below a certain high level even though they seldom get above the clouds, are better to listen to and of more use to the world than are those who soar occasionally but are apt to fall without notice. I wonder if I am wrong in thinking that a man more easily maintains a high level if he writes his sermons. There are extemporaneous preachers who sometimes carry me away completely, and sometimes don't even get hold of me. I don't seem to have observed the same variation in those who depend less upon the inspiration of the time and the place. It is a great thing to have preached the gospel for forty years and never once to have done it cheaply, foolishly, miserably.

Missionary sermons are not easy to preach, probably never have been. No more than a small minority of any congregation was ever interested in missions. If the presentation of the subject is left to the secretary of the missionary society or to the missionary on furlough, interest does not increase at any alarming rate. People feel that the secretary is a special pleader; he is paid to talk about missions. Perhaps they even know that he is in the pulpit against the preference of the pastor — for there are ministers who in spite of all their bitter experience would still rather listen to themselves than to anyone else. Some of the people absent themselves. Those who come discount what they hear, unless it is — as it often is — something that cannot be discounted. The returned missionary is sometimes a magnificent speaker, and sometimes not. Nor is it necessarily the best missionary who is the best speaker. He may for years have been accustomed to speak in some language other than English. His work may be of the unspectacular kind which lends itself but slightly to anecdotes and fetching incidents. He may be out of the habit of speaking in public, certainly to an American congregation. He may not sense at all the points at which American prejudice sticks.

The returned missionary and the secretary should be given a place in the best pulpits of the country, such as the dignity and importance of their work entitle them to. But the preacher who relies upon them to convert his people or educate them on the work of the Christian church outside of

Christendom will be disappointed. It is a thing he must do himself. If he has any gift of popular speech, any humor, any imagination, any eloquence, here is where they are called for almost more than on any other subject. Two talks a year on missions should be a minimum. Let a man speak once on foreign missions and once on home missions (begging the pardon of those who say, rightly, that the distinction between them is artificial). Let him lay hold on some grand little book, like Sam Higginbotham's *The Gospel and the Plow,* or Ray Phillips' *The Bantu are Coming,* and exploit the spectacular and practical and human stuff in it. Let him disabuse his people's minds of some of those prejudices and catchwords which are so easily caught and so unintelligently spread — such as that all religions are equally good, or that we have no moral right to impose our religion upon somebody else. Let him show how we owe to the missionaries themselves the larger part of our knowledge of religions other than Christianity. Let him tell again — most people even now have never heard it — the life story of some great missionary statesman like David Livingstone. Let him show the importance of having upon foreign soil, side by side with those Americans or Englishmen who are there to exploit the people and who often woefully misrepresent the countries from which they come, some representatives of the cultural and spiritual side of American or British civilization. Let him not evade any honest criticisms that have been made of missionary work, but let him show how much superior in educational equipment the average missionary is to the average preacher at home. Let him trace some of the bearings of missionary effort upon the cultural life of non-Christian civilizations. Let him not be afraid of misrepresenting missionary work by dwelling upon those of its features that will make the best appeal to the average hearer — such features as its schools, its hospitals and dispensaries, its work in health and sanitation; and let him do his level best with the subject, in the consciousness that it is either outside the knowledge or against the prejudices of a large proportion of his people. Let him say to himself, " At this point I am a pleader. I will not be a dishonest pleader, but I will be as forcible and persuasive a pleader as I know how to be." And let him not announce beforehand what he is going to do, lest his people treat him as they do the secretary or the missionary on furlough. Even so he will not quickly either educate or convert his people on the subject, but he will make an impression upon them, which repeated year after year will not only remold their idea of missions but enlarge and liberalize their conception of religion itself. At a missionary rally years ago I heard a returned missionary say, " There are three great American corporations in China: the Standard Oil Company, the American Tobacco Company, and the American Board; and the motto of all of them is the same, ' Let there be light.' " There cannot be any doubt about what kind of light is most needed in China, nor about the fact that people in America need light on the whole great question of missions. They need information, not of the statistical but of the human and illuminating kind. Some ministers will be too much interested in themselves and their own little job to stop to give this enlightenment to their people, but those who do give it will be greatly rewarded.

Anecdotes in general are a snare to the minister and a weariness to his congregation. A good story well told is in place now and then. There is usually a way, however, of getting the point out of a story without telling it. If, for instance, I am speaking of the evils of loose thinking I can say, " It reminds me of the story about the man in Maine. He was shingling his barn, etc." Or I can simply say, " Like the man who was shingling his barn on a very foggy day and shingled right off onto the fog." Most stories one is tempted to tell in the pulpit have a point that can be detached from the story and used by itself. Of one thing an honest minister will never be guilty: he will never tell as having happened to himself something that did not actually happen so. Not long ago I heard a preacher tell as his own personal experience a happening which, sixty years ago, I heard my father relate as having happened to someone else. If a man gets caught — and he usually will get caught — at deception in such a small matter, how will anyone believe him in greater ones? To say the least, the finer edge of sincerity is gone from him; he may not lie or steal, but there is something twisted in him. I notice that a volume of illustrations for use in sermons is about to be published; it is not a good omen.

A word of encouragement may be said, in all honesty, to the preacher who is discouraged after his Sunday morning service. If he is justified in being discouraged, let him ask himself what was wrong — for however much the congregation may be to blame the minister has to take their reaction for what it is; it is one element in his problem. If he looks for the cause of discouragement in himself, that may help him. But Sunday morning, right after church, is the time for a preacher to be discouraged. He is, or should be, tired out, "all in," not in a condition to appreciate himself or place a value upon his own work. Compliments after the sermon are often an embarrassment rather than a help. But they have one function: they dull the edge of a man's disappointment with himself for the moment, and give him time to go home and eat his dinner and take a nap and gradually work back to normal. I have not always felt discouraged after preaching. Sometimes I have felt that I have done quite well — for me, of course. But I have as often been wrong about this feeling as about the opposite one. If a man were not human you could simply tell him to "forget it." Since most preachers are human they cannot quite do this; but they can discount it, remember when they have been wrong about themselves before, try to do better, and so turn the weed into a flower.

By far the best work any preacher does is that done before his own congregation. Men who have never been invited to preach at colleges are likely to envy those who have. It is important that such preaching should be well done. The reputation of the ministry and the church may be much affected by it in the minds of the younger generation. At the same time, to travel about and give the same sermon, perhaps ten or twenty times over, to people many of whom are present under compulsion, all of whom one never saw before and will never see again, and for whom one feels no closer responsibility than the storekeeper feels for a chance customer — is certainly not the way to bring out the best in the preacher. College students are often regarded as very acute and mature. These traits they more frequently display by staying away from chapel than by any reaction to what they have heard there. Those of them who are there are not necessarily more discriminating than the members of an average congregation in an average town, while the strictly nonpastoral relation between them and the preacher of the morning precludes the best results that are to be had from preaching.

I say this by way of encouragement — and incidentally because I think it is true — to men who may have been disappointed in not being asked to do much or any "college preaching." Those who do it, of course, should be the best preachers that can be had, and should do their best. A friend of mine who was at the time a teacher in Vassar complained to me that visiting preachers did not estimate highly enough the maturity and seriousness of the congregation. She said it should be given the very best and most solid stuff the preacher could produce, whereas too many preachers seemed to think it necessary to come down to the undergraduate level. Then she added, "The man who preached this morning didn't have to come down; he was down already." College students are also people, and for the most part they need and appreciate the same kind of sermon that other folks do.

Some ministers spend a good deal of time speaking to Rotary, Kiwanis, Lions, and other service clubs. To do so occasionally is good for one. It brings one into temporary contact with men outside his own congregation, and the atmosphere of the place is likely to liven him up a bit. But it is dangerous to get a reputation for doing this kind of thing too well. One has then to do it too often. After all, it is only entertainment; one tells a few good stories, makes a casual remark or two on some public question, keeps his eye on the clock, and gets through. Once in a long while he may drop in such an assembly some seed that will come up; but most of it goes onto the rocks. The men who listen are fine men, but the time and the place are unpropitious for any results worth the time and effort of the speaker. To put it more bluntly, it is usually a waste of the preacher's time. Most men's clubs do not really need to be addressed.

If I may be so bold, I should like to speak here of my own experience in preaching a particular kind of sermon — children's sermons. Not a word was said to me about this kind of preaching in my homiletics classes in the theological school. I don't know that I was even aware that anybody ever preached children's sermons. One day, in my first pastorate, a good woman reported to me that her little daughter had said to her, " I don't see why I should go to church. I can't understand what Mr. Patton says." My sympathies were all with the little girl. But the mother also seemed to deserve some consideration. After thinking a moment I took a bold stand. I said, "Tell Barbara to be at church next Sunday and I will have a sermon just for her." That week I spent pretty nearly all my time thinking up a sermon for Barbara. What did one say to children, anyhow? I didn't know, partly I suppose because I hadn't any children. But I got something, I think a story out of a book, and laboriously made it over for Barbara. It was a somewhat sad affair, and a rather sad occasion for me. But Barbara was there — in the front seat, and another small girl with her. I gave them my children's sermon, such as it was. They seemed to like it, or at least they liked the idea that I had paid so much attention to them. They said they would be back next Sunday. They were, and there was a small boy with them.

From that time to the end of my preaching ministry I always preached a children's sermon. Such sermons came easier and easier until they were not a task but a delight to me. Something I had seen in a store window or elsewhere along the street or about town, some remark dropped in my hearing, some incident out of the newspaper, a ride on the railroad train, a happening out of my own boyhood — they seemed to buzz around me, these children's sermons, like mosquitoes in a swamp. We organized a little for them. We had the children from certain classes in the Sunday school come in and sit in the front seats. They stayed through the invocation and the Lord's Prayer, which they repeated with more gusto and fewer mistakes than the grown folks. They listened to the choir sing one anthem. Then they heard the children's sermon, and during the singing of a hymn they were excused. We never had a large number of children — some thirty or forty perhaps, not always that many; but they always listened and there was not one among them who shut his eyes or looked down his nose during the procedure. What surprised me most was that the grown folks listened too. In fact it rather bothered me sometimes that they seemed to like the children's sermon better than their own! I should be sorry to awaken mercenary motives in any preacher's heart, but years later it occurred to me to submit a bundle of these children's sermons to a publisher. He took them at once. They made the only book I ever wrote which cost me no effort and which helped to keep me off relief.

I believe this practice of preaching children's sermons was good for me and would be good for anyone, especially for one who has a tendency to be too abstract and impersonal in his preaching. His preaching to children will tend to react upon his preaching to grown folks, livening it up, taking unnecessary starch out of it. He may read Whitehead all the week, but he will not talk like Whitehead on Sunday, even in his grown-up sermon, if he preaches a children's sermon. It has the additional advantage of getting children accustomed to some part of the church service, and of making them feel that the preacher is interested in them as well as in their fathers and mothers. After all, children also are people.

There is an often used phrase whose meaning is sometimes doubtful, because more than one meaning can be put into it — the phrase "evangelical preaching." Etymologically it seems to mean gospel preaching. It is often restricted to preaching that deals primarily with the death of Jesus and that urges men to immediate repentance in the hope of eternal life. Such preaching, if rightly done, and to people who need it, is always powerful. But there is a broader meaning which the phrase should also carry. A man is not necessarily unevangelical because the doctrine of the atonement has ceased to be vital to him, nor because he bases his appeal toward the right life upon motives closer to him than his destiny in some other world. He is evangelical if he has the spirit of the gospel in him; if he is warm, sympathetic, earnest, and has the personal spiritual welfare of his hearers deeply at heart. A man may believe all the older doctrines and not be evangelical in the wider sense unless he has this spirit of the gospel. Those who have this spirit may be evangelical no matter how critical their views of the Bible or how modern their theology. In this larger sense all preaching should be evangelical.

A reasonable degree of novelty or up-to-dateness is an asset to the preacher. He is a man of his own generation. Yet the old themes, time-honored and even timeworn, are the fundamental themes. Time spent in a hunt for mere novelty is thrown away. I would even, now and then, purposely go to the other extreme and take some subject just because it is old; such subjects, for instance, as the love of God, the grace of God in Jesus Christ, salvation, redemption, faith, repentance. I would be frank about them. I would try to show what they have meant to other generations and what they ought to mean to this one. If they do not mean anything for this generation I would say so.

I would apply this same principle to texts as well as to subjects. I would take an old text that doesn't seem to belong in this generation at all — like, "Without shedding of blood there is no remission of sins." I would try to show in what circle of religious ideas such a statement would have arisen, how that circle of ideas has disappeared, and therefore how any literal application of these old words has become impossible for us. Then if there is any modicum of permanent truth in the statement I would try to show what that is. I would take the text, "God so loved the world that he gave his only-begotten Son." I would treat it frankly and from my own point of view. I would say that it is found in the Fourth Gospel, that nothing like it is found in the Synoptics, and that moreover it doesn't seem natural for Jesus thus to refer to himself in the third person, by an official title, and as if the crucifixion had already taken place. Then I would show that quite aside from the authenticity of the words ascribed to Jesus in the Fourth Gospel, these particular words are not ascribed to him there but are the statement of the author of the gospel himself. They are an interpretation of the person and work of Jesus such as would naturally have been made around the end of the first century. I would inquire into the meaning of "only-begotten" and how far that phrase means anything to us today; I would ask what eternal life means and how one may expect to get it from Jesus. I would try to give the sermon a positive conclusion, perhaps concerning the place of self-sacrifice in human life and in the divine life, thus building it up (a matter I have spoken of elsewhere) into some total view or philosophy.

I would do this with many old texts. These old texts are there. In earlier years they were the staple of the preacher's thought. The modern preacher may easily give the impression that he is afraid of them, doesn't know what to do with them, and hopes that his people have forgotten them. Meanwhile they remain, half-buried obstacles to modern views of religion. People listen to the liberal preacher, get his general point of view, probably approve of it, but still say to themselves, "What does he do with this? What can he say about that?" And generally he says nothing, and people wonder.

A vast amount of literature — nonhomiletic literature — has in times past been produced by ministers. This has included novels, poetry, and especially essays. One thinks — to put them all together indiscriminately — of Henry Van

Dyke, Edward Everett Hale, Samuel Crothers, Dean Trench, Dean Stanley, Dean Inge, Charles Kingsley, Dr. Edgar Goodspeed, Ralph Connor, Harold Bell Wright, Lloyd Douglas, and others greater and less, a very considerable company. Not every minister is a literary artist. But the ministry is a literary calling, and it is good practice for any minister to try his hand now and then at some literary effort besides sermons. Let him write an essay now and then on books, on his travels, on some aspect of current society or contemporary manners that appeals to him, and send it to a magazine. He will usually get it back, to be sure. In that case he can get much pleasure from reading the magazine which rejected it and seeing how much better his own article is than the ones that got printed. Or if, as will happen now and then, his article is printed, it will give him the harmless satisfaction of renewing his unconfessed conviction that he might have been a literary man if he had not preferred to be a preacher. Aside from either of these events the practice will react favorably upon the literary character of his work as a preacher.

CHAPTER SEVEN

THE DELIVERY OF THE SERMON

THE PROPER WAY to deliver a sermon would seem to be the way that is natural to the man who is delivering it. Yet here appears a queer thing; we all get into unnatural habits — the pulpit tone, the minor cadence, the forced smile, the awkward or nervous manipulation of the hands, and so on. And this we often do with the greatest desire to be natural and with a true hatred of anything artificial or pretended. I recall a preacher who was about as simplehearted a man as you would ever find. Any pretense, in the pulpit or out of it, was anathema to him. He couldn't have " put on " if he had tried. He once asked his wife to criticize his preaching. She demurred, but he urged her. Thus driven to it, and being a truthful woman, she said: " Lewis, you are not natural in the pulpit; not your tone, not your look, not anything about you." He was dumfounded, and at first inclined to be angry about the criticism or to deny it; he did so hate anything that was unnatural. Yet there was what his wife had said; and she was not only truthful but discriminating, and he knew it. I suppose he had got into all his unnatural habits in the early days when he was nervous and couldn't be quite natural and they had grown on him with the years. What I wish to stress here is the fact that although we are unconscious of being unnatural that is no assurance that we are not so.

The fundamental objective in delivery is force, just as it is in style — not necessarily a noisy force, nor a threatening or bullying force. The force in the delivery of a speech may be as quiet and unobtrusive as the force of the sunshine, and people may be as unconscious of it. But unless the sermon strikes home in the delivery, as it would not if it were merely read, there is nothing gained by delivering it.

To begin in the most general way, then, the preacher should always have in mind that he is going to add by his delivery to whatever force there is in the thought he has to present. It will not do for him to say to himself of some sermon he is about to deliver, " This is not much of a sermon and not worth making much effort for in the delivery." In the first place the preacher can seldom tell — in fact he generally cannot tell — which of his sermons will appeal most to his people or do them the most good. He knows which sermon he has worked hardest on, but often that proves to be the one that people do not care for. If he is a critically minded man he sees flaws in his sermon — poor arrangement of material, overdevelopment of one point or underdevelopment of another — which he would remedy if he had a few hours more before he had to go into the pulpit. Sometimes these flaws are not there; he only imagines they are because he has worked too hard and too long on the sermon; or he judges them to be there because he contrasts the sermon as it is with the one he feels he could make in its place. But whether or not he is right in his own judgment, the people have no such standard by which to judge as the preacher has. They have not worked the material over and have no idea as to what might be done with it other than what the preacher has actually done. For them at least therefore the faults which the preacher sees in the sermon are not there. They listen to it, are touched and moved by it, and get help from it. It would certainly have been a mistake for the preacher to have weakened its impressiveness by delivering it as if it were not worth delivering. He can always say to himself, " Maybe I am wrong about it. Maybe it's a good deal better than I think it is." It's a fair chance that the people will think so — and they may be right. In the second place, if he is right in his judgment that it is not much of a sermon, then there is all the greater need for the most effective delivery he can give it.

On the other hand, it will not do for the preacher to say to himself, " This is a good sermon. It has good ideas in it. It is well constructed. Whoever has any sense should be able to listen to it without much help from me " — for again he may be wrong. The sermon may seem good to him but not necessarily to the people. If it is good, why not make it better by an effective delivery? If it is not so good, why not cover up the defects which he himself does not sense by the best delivery he can muster?

In other words, of every sermon he is to preach, no matter what he thinks of it, the preacher should say, " Better or worse, this sermon is going to go over at its maximum because of the way I give it." He should no more be content with a careless or uninterested delivery than he is with a slovenly written sermon. There are men who discount whatever they say by their manner. They might as well say to the congregation, " A good sermon have I not, but such as I have give I unto thee." This is not modesty; it is the inferiority complex. And the opposite attitude is not conceit; it is only common sense. Even with a good sermon, the effect of a poor delivery is like that of a sign I used to see in New England: "Hood's sarsaparilla makes the weak strong." It was painted on a barn that was falling down. I looked at it and thought, "If it can't hold the barn up, what can it do for me?"   And I resolved never to buy any of it. Let us start with the fact that every delivery, like every sermon, should be the best a man can give.

What gives force to delivery? A good voice, to be sure. A bad voice — rasping, nasal, and unpleasant — is a handicap, but one that can be largely overcome. Nor is there any one kind of voice that has all of the advantages and none of the disadvantages of voices in general. The big, resonant, sonorous bass voice is easy to listen to, but on the other hand it is apt to be monotonous, unflexible, and incapable of rendering the finer distinctions of thought and feeling. It may just boom along on one deep note, like the voice of a bullfrog. The voice of higher pitch and slighter volume may, simply as a voice, be less easy to listen to; but it may and usually does have greater flexibility, greater facility in the rendering of fine shades of thought and feeling, and even better carrying power.

I am not an expert in the matter of voice placement, but I do know some things about it just from having used my own voice so much in public. One can, for one thing, cultivate the use of the middle register of his voice. Its original timbre he cannot perhaps greatly change, but even in this particular he can, by listening carefully to himself and through long practice, cut down considerably a nasal or throaty quality.

What however he can always do is cultivate the median register. If his voice is pitched low he need not always let it growl along underground. If he can cover an octave and a half in singing, why should he restrict himself to three notes in speaking? If his voice is naturally high he need not let it squeak along at its topmost pitch. He can bring it down half an octave or more. In order to place the voice in its middle register, where it will not be tiresome by being either too high or too low, no special knowledge of the voice or instruction in its use is required. All that is necessary is that the preacher listen critically to himself and do his best to improve.

A little knowledge of the voice and its use does help a speaker in the control of his breath. The throat is like a small-scale organ of which the chest is the air chamber. It is the air passing through the windpipe that makes the sound. Young preachers are likely to fill up this air chamber by taking a good long breath, and then speaking as long as there is any air left to pass through the pipe. By so doing they generally begin with a strong voice after a good breath, and peter out as the wind begins to fail. This practice results in a rhythmic alternation between loud and soft, strong and weak sounds, sometimes culminating in an involuntary and ill-timed pause and a gasp for breath. The remedy is very simple, though one may have to go to a singing teacher to learn how to apply it. A speaker must know how to " handle his breath " — how to keep the column of air moving smoothly through his pipe at whatever rate he wants, with nothing to suggest to his hearers the fear that it may give out. He should " throw his chest out," for the chest is to the voice what the sounding board is to the organ. Any sound that comes from a collapsed or deflated wind box is a feeble and discouraging sound, no matter how noble the word it utters.

But better than to tell a man to " throw his chest out " is to tell him to hold his belly in. He may fill his lungs as full as he needs to for ordinary breathing purposes by merely drawing the air into them till he has enough to live on for the moment. But filling the lungs doesn't necessarily throw the chest out; what does that is pulling in the diaphragm. The muscles that control breathing are not in the lungs but below them. To have control of one's diaphragm and to use it to send the air through the lungs without letting the lungs collapse in the process — that is the secret of a good voice, or rather the habit. For it is a habit, and one which many public speakers form naturally and without conscious effort; but many do not, and need advice. The vocal teacher is the natural person to give such advice.

Theoretically the thing should be clear enough. The throat is the organ pipe, the chest the sounding box and air reservoir; the diaphragm controls the column of air passing through the windpipe, the chest not collapsing as the air passes through, not even when the supply of air gets low, but serving the purpose of a sounding board — this is the physical apparatus of the speaker, in which not only the throat or the lungs or any other one small part of him is involved, but the whole. It is this physical habit in speaking that puts in his control all the voice the Lord gave him. When a man speaks in this way he has himself physically and nervously in hand and uses himself, so to say, for the purpose of speaking. There is a lot to speaking that is merely physical. A man cannot speak forcibly without the expenditure of much physical and nervous energy. If his body is relaxed, flabby, at ease, his utterance will be feeble. Perhaps the first, most general and inclusive rule for forcible public utterance is learning how to enlist and utilize the whole body as an aid, abettor and implement of the vocal apparatus. Let the whole man speak.

In speaking of pulpit style I said that one element of force is clearness. This is as true of the voice as of the sentence. What the short word and the clear arrangement are to the literary style, articulation is to the voice. The listener should hear easily as he should understand easily. Any effort wasted upon catching the mere words is so much attention diverted from the sense of what is being said. When I listen to a sermon I not only want to hear, but I want to hear with entire ease. This is not a matter of mere loudness of speaking, though of course a man must speak loud enough to be heard, but it is more a matter of enunciation, distinctness. The volume of sound needs to be large enough only to reach the listener without fading out at any point. But words that needlessly run into each other, consonants indistinctly pronounced, slovenly enunciation, give an uncertain sound at which nobody prepares himself for battle.

Men are naturally very different in the way they enunciate; or probably it is more true to say that they are very different in their habits. One carries over from his childhood the habit of distinct or slovenly enunciation which he got at home. It is seldom a matter of physical capacity or the reverse. All normal persons are equipped with the tools for speaking distinctly; but one may have made such bad use of them that when he enters the ministry, or even after he has been in it for some time, it may be necessary for him to put himself through a course of discipline. Distinctness of course does not come from the throat; the volume of sound comes from there. Distinctness comes from the way one uses his lips, the tip of his tongue, and his teeth. At the place where the sound finally issues, made into words, is where the distinctness or the indistinctness is manufactured.

If a speaker has difficulty with his articulation, let him go to hear a great singer. Let him carry his opera glasses with him, sit up close, and notice what she does. When she wants more volume she does not — as the speaker often does when he wants to be emphatic — squeeze up her throat and push; she just opens it up and lets more air come through it. The vowels carry the stream of sound for her, and she dwells upon them, her language almost floating in them. Her mouth is wide open so that this stream of vowel-sound can come out without obstruction or impediment. But when she comes to a consonant, she makes the sound click with the tip of her tongue against her teeth, or narrows it down to a point with her lips. In whatever way is appropriate to the particular sound she cuts those consonants off sharp, snips them like a knitter snipping off her thread with a pair of shears. The volume of sound goes on almost without interruption, but what happens in it as she passes from one word to another is as perfectly distinct as if there had been no sound before it or were none after it. Let a moving picture be taken, a closeup, of her face as she sings, then let it be stopped as she is in the middle of making some consonantal sound. You would hardly believe that anyone would ever have concentrated so much action, so much decision, so much contortion almost, in the muscles of the lips and around the mouth. There is nothing unnatural or unhandsome about this movement as she sings, because she passes rapidly from one action to another. For that reason, as you watch her singing, unless you watch her very carefully and try in imagination to isolate one and then another facial expression from the whole of which it is so small a part, you do not realize what she does. When with the help of the opera glasses you do see what she does, you get an idea of what the speaker also must do if he is to speak with perfect distinctness.

It is as I said a matter of control, habitual control, and use to the uttermost of the muscles of the mouth and lips with which the consonantal sounds are made. Some men hardly open their mouths at all in ordinary conversation and seem to have no particular control of the muscles of their lips.   It is not easy to say what advice should be given to such men if they are going to be preachers, except that it can hardly be too drastic. They might stand in front of the looking glass and make faces at themselves, deliberately contorting their lips as extravagantly as they can, doing it over and over again till they are lip-conscious. They might even practice osculation — anything to bring to life that part of the face which alone is instrumental in the formation of perfectly distinct consonantal sounds. Clearness is the first element in force; and distinctness of enunciation, after the very primitive matter of making oneself heard at all has been mastered, is the first element in clearness.

Primarily, it is the thought that has the force. It is for the delivery to render that thought with perfect clearness, and with such helps as it can give. One such help is variation in the rate of speaking, corresponding to what is being said. In conversation some things are said rapidly, some are said slowly. The distinction between them is drawn instinctively and to the listener the difference in the rate of utterance vitally affects the significance. Yet often a sermon is delivered practically without any variation in rate of utterance. This is perhaps sometimes due to the fact that there is nothing in the thought to compel or even suggest such variation. But it also often occurs in spite of the fact that the thought does call for variation of utterance. The introduction should be simple in thought and hence moderate in movement; nobody likes to be jerked into maximum speed at one stroke. But as the sermon proceeds, if there is nothing in it that suggests a more rapid rate of delivery, or nothing that impels one to the greater solemnity that comes from conscious and intentional slowness of utterance, there cannot be very much of anything in it.

Perhaps that is too strong a statement. A sermon might, I suppose, be made up of one continuous argument or one continuous something which gathered no momentum and ought therefore to be uttered at one rate, like the multiplication table or vocal exercises timed to the metronome. In that case it would have about the same appeal as these. But in a sermon that has any human appeal whatever, there is a time to go slow, and an emphasis which comes from an obvious retardation and can hardly be got in any other way. And there are other times when for its adequate utterance or appreciation the thought demands that the speaker hurry; and if he does not hurry he shows that he does not appreciate its quality. As Rosalind asks Celia ten distinct questions about Orlando, and says, " Answer me in one word "; or as Cleopatra says to the messenger from Italy,

> Ram thou thy fruitful tidings in mine ears
> That long time have been barren,

there are things we " can't wait to hear."   They should be said as fast as they can be understood.   The only limit on their speed is the facility of the speaker's tongue.   Nothing gives more of an impression of monotony even to an otherwise good sermon than delivery of it at one uniform rate.   Indeed one suspects that its matter must be monotonous, else it would neither suggest nor suffer such a delivery.   A preacher who has prepared anything to say that has any variety of meaning or importance will naturally appreciate this variety, and will instinctively vary the rate of his utterance to suit what he is saying — at least this statement would be true if all preachers spoke as naturally and instinctively in the pulpit as they do out of it.   But since they do not, and since it is almost impossible to do so, nothing remains for the preacher but to watch himself in this matter, as he has to do in so many others.

Something very like this matter of rate, and equally important though not generally recognized, is that of pause.   In all dramatic literature much use is made of the pause as a means of heightening the impressiveness of what follows. The actor, much more intent than the preacher is or should be upon extracting the uttermost from every word, makes use of the pause in a way that should be suggestive to the preacher even if he cannot wholly imitate it.   In the scene in *Macbeth* which immediately follows the murder of Duncan, where

Macbeth and Lady Macbeth are talking of what has happened and there comes a knocking at the door, few readers would fail to feel the necessity of the pause, and certainly no actor would fail to employ it. To hurry through the passage, and to allow, for instance, the words " Hark! More knocking: get on your nightgown " to flow along smoothly without a pause, is to rob them of half their natural significance. One of the most impressive moments in choral music is that instant just before the final hallelujah in the " Hallelujah Chorus," when the singers are breathless, the organ or the orchestra still, and the conductor poised with uplifted baton and with bated breath for the signal that is to bring the last grand burst of music. Not only does the last hallelujah gain half its magnificence from the pause that precedes it, but there even seems to be music of a peculiar kind in the pause itself. The preacher is not primarily a dramatic artist; he works with ideas rather than with sounds or colors. But in many sermons there will be dramatic moments, and many of these will be likely to escape the listeners entirely if the preacher has no idea of the value of the pause or no habit of using it.

I have even known a preacher who made a most effective use of the pause, not before he said something important, but after it. When something he had said had deeply stirred his hearers, while they were yet in a mood either to be carried to some greater height or to stand tiptoe where they were, this preacher would often pause a moment. He seemed in fact to hesitate. I presume that is what he was doing. He was asking himself whether what he had just said had gone home to the depths of his hearers' hearts, or whether he should give them another thrust. Whenever you heard him pause thus you knew he had just said something which to him at least was of unusual significance, and you thought over what had been said in the light of the speaker's own feeling, and it sank deeper. For him to have rushed on to the utterance of something else would have belittled his significant utterance.

The more common use of the pause is simpler and less dramatic than these occasional uses, but not less important. The pause is, to the speaker, what the division into paragraphs is to the writer. In spite of all the books I have read I am still more or less dismayed when I turn a page that has no paragraphs on it. If the writer knows what he means by paragraphs and uses them when he should, this seems to mean that here is a page on which I shall have no breathing spell whatever. I must stretch my mind from its first sentence to its last. Now what a paragraph on the printed page does for the reader, the pause does for the hearer. It gives him time to breathe and say to himself, " I am not sunk yet."

Moreover, a paragraph on a page usually indicates a break and generally a more or less definite transition in the thought. When the reader comes to one he pauses and says to himself, " Here we turn a corner." It helps him to know where he is. This is what the pause does for the listener. A sermon may be arranged with perfect logic and may pass from one item to the next just as it should; and all these turnings and passings and transitions may be quite thrown away on the listener because the speaker never pauses nor hesitates nor betrays in any way by his voice and manner what his thought is doing. Few devices in public speech are more important and few are more often neglected than the pause. In conversation, or still more in a lively argument, it is not so. There, we pause where we ought to. If we are standing we shift from one foot to the other, or we rise if we are sitting, or we shake our heads, or we make a gesture; in some one of innumerable ways we indicate that we have finished one thing and are passing on to something else. Here again, if a man spoke as naturally and with as little self-consciousness in the pulpit as he does in the club or on the golf grounds, it would be unnecessary even to mention all this. But since he does not, it is necessary for him to watch himself and see that he does what he should. Right delivery will come to him with experience, but not unless he is on the lookout for it.

Concerning this matter of the pause, I recently read in Somerset Maugham's "Theater" the advice of one old actor to a younger one. He said, "Never pause unless you have a reason to. But when you pause, pause as long as you can." Rightly interpreted I suppose that is good advice. If you don't pause long enough to let people know that you have paused, you have merely wasted a moment; but if you pause so long that people fear you have forgotten what is to follow, that is equally bad. The preacher should be able to tell how long the pause should be. There is a look in people's faces that seems to say, "Yes; that's so"; and as long as that look remains, the pause is evidently doing its work. But when that look is supplanted by one which says just as plainly, "Well, we have that. What next?" it is time to go on.

But I really quoted this statement from "Theater" to say that a preacher, since in his own way he is or tries to be an artist, should hear every great artist he can — every great singer, though he himself is not a singer; every great violinist, though he himself is not a violinist. Hearing great interpreters does something to his emotional setup that is good for him and that he often very much needs; it gives him a standard and an ideal to reach toward. But of all the artists he can hear, the actor is generally the one from whom he can learn the least. The stage deals in illusion, the pulpit in reality. The business of the actor, as the same character in " Theater " says, is not to be natural but to seem natural; the business of the preacher is to be what he seems.

There is one question that has probably received more attention than it deserves — whether a man should speak without notes, with notes, or with a manuscript. Let him find his own way and use it. However, if he speaks wholly without manuscript or notes of even the briefest sort, that fact has no bearing upon the value of writing out his sermon beforehand. And also, it is possible, if a man does not find himself able to command a good style in the more extemporaneous manner, to give a sermon from manuscript with practically all the simplicity, directness, and force of the extemporaneous method; or if that statement is too strong, at least a sermon can be given from manuscript — not *read* in the hearing of the people but *delivered* to a congregation — with so much force and directness that nothing will seem to be lacking in those respects and the greater literary power will more than make up for the defect in delivery, if there is any.

I said, let a man find his own way of speaking and follow it. Yet it is a mistake to be too much tied to any one way. A preacher will often be called upon to speak where neither manuscript nor notes are acceptable, and then it is a pity if he cannot do reasonably well without either of them. He will also be called upon to speak where he must absolutely put the most he can say into the shortest time and with the greatest skill and art; and he will be a very rare man if he can do that in a purely extempore way. Moreover, each of these ways of speaking reacts upon the others. The man who speaks without notes will deliver his manuscript sermon with less bondage to his written words. The man who uses his manuscript in the pulpit will have a certain ideal of terseness and literary finish which the man who never does so will not so easily have. If it is a pity to have to write out a mere prayer meeting talk, it is equally a pity to talk upon some great occasion loosely, ramblingly, and too long.

Since I am here speaking about delivery and not about style, all I want to say is that a man may get pulpit force in any of these ways of speaking. For many generations it was assumed that all sermons should be written and read from the manuscript. It was in this manner that the New England preachers of a few generations ago almost always preached. But it was a mistake to assume that that was the only way to preach. Nowadays it is thought that for the preacher to use a manuscript is a sign of timidity or weakness of some sort, and that the only real way to preach is to get up and talk — and this is equally a mistake.

There is a delivery that goes naturally with the kind of sermon a man is preaching. Earnestness is always presupposed. If the preacher doesn't care about what he is saying, why should I? Yet earnestness may show itself in different ways. I remember a student who preached in class a sermon from the text, " The servant of the Lord should not strive, but be gentle towards all." The instructor's comment upon it was,

"It was a sermon on gentleness delivered in a very fierce manner." Yet earnestness, as I said, is always in order; and earnestness always costs something. It costs intellectual conviction to begin with, and after that it costs nervous and physical energy. I remember the time when it first occurred to me that I must put physical energy into my preaching. The preacher faces a crisis every time he stands before a congregation; and though it is not primarily a physical crisis, yet no mere mental keenness nor perfection of yesterday's preparation will by themselves bring him through it. He must be keyed up to it, keyed up all over, in his nerves and in his muscles, so that when he gets through he feels as if he had done a day's work. I should say — only I feel as if someone had already said it — that if he isn't tired when he gets through preaching it is a sure sign that his congregation will be. A man must square himself for preaching as he would for any other struggle. A loose-hanging body, a pair of semi-collapsed lungs, hands that hang wooden, a stance with one leg and foot unused, will never bring him through. He must bring to the front all the resources he has; and we of today should not need to be told that the line between the mental and the physical is a thin one. He must preach with his whole personality, and his body is part of his personality; it is the part that embodies the rest of it. In his study on Saturday the preacher may relax his body while he uses his mind, but in his pulpit on Sunday he must forget any distinction between his body and his mind and use them both to the utmost. In the pulpit flesh helps soul as much as soul helps flesh — or whatever it was that Browning said.

Here is a place, of course, where temperament counts.

There are a few men — and some of them get into the ministry — who do not warm up before a congregation. The more
people there are in front of them the colder they get. They
seem to say, " Here are four hundred against one. What can
a man do?" And so they do as little as possible. We should
be grateful that not many of us are so made. Most of us
when we confront a congregation say to ourselves — not consciously of course — " I will preach to you in love. My heart
is warm toward you. There is no quarrel between us; but
you've got to take this just the same." It is a nervous and
mental and equally a physical reaction, and it will show itself
in the muscular and nervous energy a man puts into his
speech. He will not generally realize this while he is speaking. His people may say to him after the sermon, " How
easily you speak, as if you were making no effort at all." But
he knows better; he knows that after he has got home you
could almost wring him out like a sponge. It should be so.

What can a man do about mannerisms — a habit perhaps
of rising on his toes and dropping back again, the too ministerial tone, the smile that threatens not to come off? Get
someone to tell him about them, for he himself will never
realize that he has them. If God has been good enough to
give him a wife who is not afraid of him, and who does not
think he is perfect as he is, let him ask her; or let him ask
someone else whom he can continue to love notwithstanding
criticism. If a teacher of elocution, a good sensible one, happens to attend his services let him ask him; or better still, let
him go to such a teacher, if he knows one, and hire him to
come to church some Sunday, and so put the matter on a com-
mercial and off the personal basis.

This is one of the things a teacher of homiletics is supposed to do for his pupils. Up to a point he can do it. The trouble is that most men get their bad pulpit habits after they leave the theological school. They get them in those first few months or years in which they are still nervous before a congregation and do many things that they not only ought not to have done but that they didn't know they were doing. And though bad habits seem often to stick tighter than good ones, the man who retains the ambition to be as good a speaker as he can be is never too old to improve. The trouble with many a preacher is, he doesn't know what his bad habits are.

There are some words that are a terror to the public speaker. "Diocesan" is such a one. Outside the Episcopal pulpit one may perhaps never have to use it. It is part of the price a man pays for belonging to the true church. But a word like "inexplicable" even a Baptist or a Congregationalist might want to use. Such words cost more than they are worth; the strain of getting the teeth and the tongue successfully around them is too great. Some speakers relieve themselves of the difficulty by putting the accent on "plic," where as a matter of fact it logically belongs; but it is better to think of some other word to use. "Unexplainable" is a better word — better not merely because you can say it more easily, but because its accent falls upon the root of the word, where it ought to be; also because there is such a word as "explain" but no such word as "explic." I am speaking of the matter from the point of view not of style but of ease of utterance. Words that hinder the force of delivery are as bad as those that make an unwarranted draft on the hearer's attention.

As a final word on this matter of delivery it should once

more be said that preaching is an art and is learned by practice. Most young preachers are too tame. They stand too much like the old-fashioned wooden Indian in front of the cigar store. They make few gestures. Those they do make they usually have to make intentionally and consciously, which of course spoils them. They shift their position with too much difficulty, as if they said to themselves, "It is time to move." In short they are too stiff. This is entirely natural and unavoidable, a result simply of the fact that they are still new at their work. They are too much impressed by the time, the place and the congregation, and have too little confidence in themselves. In most cases time is a sufficient remedy, as it is the only one. The pulpit ceases to be a new glove that pinches. One finds his freedom in it and the naturalness that comes with freedom. Let the young minister preach only what he is interested in, what he believes with his whole heart, what he can throw himself into; let him keep his lungs full and his diaphragm in and his eye upon the man in the back seat; let him steer away from such bad speaking habits as anyone may tell him about; let him be intent upon getting the truth he has thought out and brought to his congregation across to them in the most forcible way he can — and he will be a good speaker; his own kind of speaker — why indeed should he want to be some other kind? — but a good speaker.

As I come to the end of this book I am conscious of the omission from it of some things that are said, and properly, in most books of its kind. They concern the motives that lead a man into the ministry and the personal religious life that sustains him in it. Though motives are always mixed in all of us, few men go into the ministry with any predominance of selfish aims. Those who do will fail — inevitably and miserably fail, as they ought to. They may succeed in getting prominent churches and a wide hearing; but they will fail in their own spirits, and that is the only kind of failure that should hurt anyone.

Yet there are some selfish, or at least self-regarding, motives that are proper in the ministry, and more likely to be realized there than almost anywhere else. One of these is the opportunity for self-improvement by reading, study, and thought about great things. Another is the joy of artistic creation. To make anything that will hold together, that will work, that will go, even if it is ugly, is in itself a joy. But artistic creation, the creation of something that not merely has " significant form " and gives you pleasure as you look at it or hear it, but that seems to you to reveal in miniature some of those principles of unity, coherence and meaning upon which the universe itself is constructed — that is a real and an inalienable joy. Not every preacher can be a great artist; not every artist in any field of creativeness can be a great artist; but every artist can be a true artist — the preacher among the rest. However far short the preacher may fall in artistry, if he has succeeded up to the limit that God imposed upon him when He made him, he will find in his heart a satisfaction compared to which all compliments of the most appreciative congregation, all reputation, all fame if he gets any, are tame and tasteless. It is a joy that pertains to himself and that piles up in himself, but a joy that links him with all creators and with the Creator.

I push this matter one step further by saying that what every man is after in this world is to leave some impression of himself upon it — to make in it somewhere a dent that can be seen; to twist it this way or that nearer to the heart's desire, and not to leave it without having communicated to it some part of that which God has given to him; to make his own thoughts a part of the equipment of other people, and his own mind part of the minds of other people; to influence the course of some other individual lives, perhaps in a small way the course of the common life, so that the world will not be quite the same as if he had not been in it — something like this is the aim, conscious or unconscious, of every human being. A man's personality is given him so that he may communicate it. If it isn't communicated it is at best partly wasted. Every man feels this to be so.

The more conscious his aim, and the more a man is intent upon leaving a good mark on the world and not a bad one, the more of a man he is. Some men accomplish this universal human purpose in one way and some in another. The architect does it through the kind of buildings he puts up, leaving behind him a better popular taste — a taste more like his own, and thus something of himself. The thinker does it by his thought, the businessman by his fortune and the methods of its making, the statesman by his laws, other men by the use of other instruments or tools. The preacher does it by the spoken word. To what purpose he does it depends on the character of the words he speaks. But as to the mere satisfaction of doing it in this way rather than in some other the universal tribute paid to the orator testifies pretty clearly. "Whoso can speak well is a man," said Luther. "If ever a woman feels proud of her lover, it is when she sees him as a successful public speaker," wrote Harriet Beecher Stowe. Both these statements may be exaggerations, but neither is without basis in the common feeling about such things. Whoever learns to speak well has opened for himself a door into an almost inexhaustible delight.

This is putting the matter on its merely egoistic and therefore its lowest terms. Even so, in a world where personal satisfaction cannot be wholly disregarded and is often an index of something better than itself, it need not be despised. It is doubtful if any successful preacher, no matter how unselfish or how contemptuous of mere personal success — Savonarola, Brooks, Chrysostom, Jesus himself — has ever been able to exclude from his soul the joy that instinctively comes from the ability to sway people by public utterance.

But when one gives himself to a cause which he feels to be the best in the world, then this mere pleasure, half egoistic and half physical as it is, gives way to a deep spiritual satisfaction. The ambassador for Jesus Christ has some part of the dignity that belongs to his Master. When a man speaks for God, and speaks a true word of God, God speaks in him, and without any spiritual pride the man may feel the blessedness of that fact. Few men in any other calling have the opportunity which the minister has of improving themselves intellectually and spiritually; few have any such opportunity to get inside the hearts and lives of so many good people. The ministry is a great calling. If it cannot always be greatly served, it can at least be served always honestly, faithfully, gratefully, and up to the limit of one's power.

INDEX

ACKNOWLEDGMENTS

The author hereby makes grateful acknowledgment of his indebtedness to the following publishers for permission to quote from volumes issued by them:

To The Macmillan Company, from *Inductive English Composition,* by W. W. Dodd.

To Harper and Brothers, from *When Christ Passes By,* by Walter Russell Bowie; *Throne Rooms,* by Gaius Glenn Atkins; *Let's Build a New World,* by Burris Jenkins; *The Story of Religions,* by Wm. R. Sweet; *The Way of Faith,* by Joseph R. Sizoo; *Toward Discovering a Religion,* by John Howland Lathrop; *Thunder Over Sinai,* by Edwin McNeil Poteat, Jr.

To E. P. Dutton, from *The Flowering of New England,* by Van Wyck Brooks.

To the University of Chicago Press, from *Preaching on Church and Community Occasions,* by Ozora Davis; *Studies in Logical Theory,* by John Dewey.

To Charles Scribner's Sons, from *Jesus Came Preaching,* by George A. Buttrick.

To Harcourt, Brace and Company, from *Best Sermons of 1925.*